GRACE
IN A
SHATTERED PLACE

Embracing God's Presence in the
Middle of Life's Broken Pieces

STEPHANIE L. MCWHORTER

authorHOUSE®

AuthorHouse™
1663 Liberty Drive
Bloomington, IN 47403
www.authorhouse.com
Phone: 1 (800) 839-8640

Scripture taken from the King James Version of the Bible.

Published by AuthorHouse   07/21/2017

ISBN: 978-1-5246-9633-7 (sc)
ISBN: 978-1-5246-9631-3 (hc)
ISBN: 978-1-5246-9632-0 (e)

Library of Congress Control Number: 2017909272

Print information available on the last page.

THE HOLY BIBLE, NEW INTERNATIONAL VERSION®, NIV® Copyright © 1973, 1978, 1984, 2011 by Biblica, Inc.® Used by permission. All rights reserved worldwide.

Scripture taken from the NEW AMERICAN STANDARD BIBLE®, Copyright © 1960,1962,1963,1968,1971,1972,1973,1975,1977,1 995 by The Lockman Foundation. Used by permission.

Scripture taken from the King James Version of the Bible.

CONTENTS

PREFACE

I was so tired of hearing that there was a rainbow after every storm and that the greatest victory always came after the greatest defeat. Enough. What about when the storm never seems to end? Where is the rainbow? Where is the victory?

I didn't want to hear that I was going to make it through. I didn't want to hear that God was on my side. I didn't want another person to tell me that if I kept praising God, He would come through for me. I had been believing all those things and I had yet to see a rainbow or experience a great victory.

After consecutive trials hit my life, I didn't want to hear another spiritual cliché. I wanted to hear real. I wanted to hear from a real person that loved Jesus, but had felt forsaken. I wanted to speak to someone that felt abandoned, rejected, and alone. I wanted to hear from someone that feared it was their lot in life to face every problem in a cave of darkness.

If I could just hear their voice, feel their pain, and listen to their story, then maybe I could find my way out of this deep despair and despondency. Maybe. But, I needed to hear it from someone who had been there. Words from anyone else just wouldn't do.

Sure. Others meant well. But the depth of my pain had become unresponsive to hope. And the brokenness of my heart was too fragile to hear admonishments from others who seemed to have no broken places in theirs.

I hadn't given up on better. I hadn't settled for defeat. But I felt stuck. Familiar with darkness and blinded to light.

If you feel this way or if you have ever felt this way, I'd like to take a moment to introduce myself and to share my story. My name is Stephanie, and I understand you. I have been there. As I write this, I am there. I feel your heart and I want to let you know that you are not alone. You are not going through this storm by yourself. You are not without an anchor and you are not without a friend.

Don't lose me at that last sentence. My utmost desire is that you finish this book with a perspective about grace and trials that you may not have had when you first started reading it. That's the reason I wrote it. Still, I promise that our journey together will not consist of empty words like "Stick with Jesus and everything will be okay."

Listen. Everything really will be okay. Nonetheless, I will keep to my promise. I won't just leave you with fancy words you have heard before while you grasp for answers. You've heard enough fancy words. Now, it's time for some real truth.

This book will allow us to struggle through the hard questions together. And yes, we will talk about why it seems that this faith thing works for others, but doesn't seem to be working for us. We'll become friends. We'll cry together and we will get up together.

I want you to know that you are not a weak Christian because you find it difficult to "fake it until you make it," or "smile through your trial." You are not weak in faith if you feel that life has beaten you down and even God has left you for dead. You are simply living your life by grace and there is beauty in the place that you are in right now!

I pray that as you read these pages you will see yourself. And I pray that you will be encouraged to endure your storm knowing that even when this verse too seems like a cliché, it is as true for your life as it is for mine.

> *For we know that all things work together for the good of those*
> *who love God and are called according to His purpose.*
>
> *Romans 8:28*

INTRODUCTION

While brainstorming for the perfect book title, I had a few conversations with my mother. One of the most memorable conversations went something like this. "So, have you come up with a title yet?" my mom asked. "Yes," I responded. "Grace in a Shattered Place." "You mean, Grace FROM a Shattered Place?" my mom retorted back. "Nooo," I said speaking a little louder as if I hadn't been clear the first time. I announced my book title to her a second time adding emphasis on the word "in". "Grace **in** a Shattered Place."

I have to preface this next part by telling you that I am a preacher's kid. Not just a preacher's kid, though. I am also a preacher's grandkid, a preacher's cousin, and a preacher's great niece. I could go further down the line, but you get the point. Sermonettes and sermons run deep in my family. We get sermons about dirty dishes, life changes, bad attitudes, and the list goes on. That's just my family. We preach. About *everything*.

So, as my mom heard me repeat my title a second time, I knew a sermon was forthcoming. "I think it should be "Grace **from** a Shattered place," she said. Then, she went on to give me a sermon that lasted for about two hours.

Okay. So maybe it was a five-minute sermon, but still, you get the point.

"Grace helps us to get up from our broken places," she said. "We are not supposed to stay down, but we are supposed to get up so we can help somebody else."

I agreed with her. She was right. We are not created to live in a place of brokenness. We are purposed to rise from broken places and help others. But it's this very truth that makes it hard for the person facing an avalanche of tragedy to feel like they matter, belong, and have something to contribute when they are facing a whirlwind of pain and disappointment. How can they possibly be of help to someone else when they are so hurt, so disappointed, and broken? These were feelings I wanted to combat, not further perpetrate.

So, I tried my second title on my mom. "What about 'When God sends grace instead of change?'" I asked. "Doesn't grace cause change?" she asked. Here we go again! Theological sermon number two! No, really. Again, I saw her point. Grace inspires us to change. Even when grace is an agent to cover us in sin, it should prompt us to be better and live better. Grace does not come to enable us to remain as we are. All of that is true, but that wasn't where I was headed! I wasn't trying to talk about the ending result of grace. Instead, I wanted to talk about the disappointment that we oftentimes incur before we recognize the presence of grace. How do we deal with that sting? That ache? That devastation?

"I don't want to write a book about change and getting up from defeat," I shared with my mom. "There are plenty of books out there like that. I want to write a book about embracing the dark places of life and learning to recognize God's grace in the darkness and not just on the other side."

So many people write about being on the other side of brokenness and finding their place of joy. Just the same, there are a plethora of resources about grief, loneliness, and depression. If you name it, there's probably a resource list for it, but there are very few resources for those struggling in the middle. People in the middle are too determined to stay down, but too broken to completely be up. So, they struggle in a place of unrest vacillating between pain and purpose, hurt and healing, loss and restoration.

Don't get me wrong. With the likes of the internet and social media these days, you can pretty much find a support group for just about anything. The people I am writing to don't usually fit into support groups, though. They don't want sympathy, they want healing. They refuse to park their lives where they have been temporarily stopped, but they aren't really sure how to get to their next point. Their hearts are still broken. They are still shaken to their core. They don't want to stay in, but they can't figure out how to get out.

If you are reading this thinking "Hey! This sounds a lot like me!" Let me let you in on a little secret. I **am** you. And this book is for you.

This is not a book written by someone who has been there. This is a book purposely written by someone who is there. Stuck right dab in the middle with you! This book won't preach to you about getting over it. It will encourage you to walk through it.

By the way, in case you're wondering, I eventually won my mom over and she has been my biggest supporter from the day that I told her I was writing this book. I love you, mom!

SECTION 1

SHATTERED PLACES

CHAPTER 1

A BROKEN SPIRIT

Psalms 51:17

A sacrifice to God is an afflicted spirit: a contrite and
humbled heart, O God, thou will not despise.
Douay-Rheims Bible

What is Brokenness?

Brokenness is not depression and it is not the result of trouble. Brokenness is a heart submitted to God in the midst of trouble. Brokenness is not tears during a worship song on a Sunday morning. It is allowing God to speak to your spirit however He chooses and whenever He chooses. It is not sorrow, it is repentance. It is not an emotion, but a position.

You may be in a difficult season in life, but if you are walking in bitterness and refusing to seek God for healing, purpose, and restoration, you are not broken. You are in rebellion. Psalms 51:3 does not say that our rebellion is a sacrifice to God, but our brokenness. Check your posture. Are you yielding to God or trying to flee from Him? We cannot expect to reap the benefits of restoration when we refuse to embrace the process of brokenness.

True brokenness opens the closet of your heart and allows God to walk in and yank out the things that He does not see as fitting. Don't be alarmed if He starts to pull at some of your favorites.

During this process, you may look at the issues from the closet of your heart in disgust and wonder how you could have ever worn such raggedness. Don't stay there. Remember that this is a process and the end result is God's beauty for your rags. Stay with Him and let Him give you a makeover!

The good news is that you can still be used by God while He is perfecting and refining you. You do not have to be perfect. So many times, we look at others and think that they have it all together because they have different struggles than we do. We are all struggling. Some struggles may be a little more painful than others and some struggles may be a little more difficult. Some struggles may even be public while others are private, but we all have struggles.

This is why it is never wise to compare. Whether you are comparing physical anatomy, careers, bank accounts, relationships, or finances; the process is the same. We are always looking at the best of someone else and using it as a measuring stick to evaluate the sum of our whole person. We have no clue what others look at in our lives wishing they could have in theirs. That spiritual giant you admire still has insecurities. They still have family pressures and work stress. And whether you believe it or not, they still have areas in their life that God is perfecting.

When we choose to focus on our broken places comparing them to someone else's whole areas, we make a conscious choice to ignore the things that are presently beautiful in our lives. We aren't just telling ourselves that we are not enough, we are telling God that He is not enough.

Imagine a conversation with God that goes like this. "God, I have been single a woman for ten years and everyone else around me is married. There must be something wrong with how you made me. I can't be happy living as a single woman. You are not enough."

Or "God, I have struggled with my weight all of my life. I am giving up on ever achieving a healthy weight. I have a friend that weighs 100 pounds less than I do and she has had five kids. I don't feel like I measure up to other mothers that manage to take care of themselves and their children. I will never truly be happy with myself until I have the body that I want. You are not enough."

I wonder how God would feel on the other side of that conversation when He intricately took the time to make us and design us so perfectly. He breathed His life into every detail of our being. He formed us, knew us, loved us then, and loves us now. (Genesis 1: 26-27) How could what He's given us not be enough? How could He not be enough?

Then God said, "Let us make man in our image, after our likeness,
and let them have dominion over the fish of the sea, and over
the birds of the air, and over the livestock, and over all the earth,
and over every creeping thing that creeps on the earth."

So God created man in His own image;
in the image of God He created him;
male and female He created them.

(Genesis 1: 26-27)

Putting our thoughts and feelings in a frame that tells God He is not enough really calls us to the carpet, especially if we say that we love

Him with our whole hearts. It becomes a painstaking thought to think that the creator of every single good and perfect living and breathing thing got to us and said, "I'm not really sure I care much about this one! I'll just give her whatever I've got left and keep it moving!"

If we know that God really didn't just pass us over, could there be something that we are missing? Is it possible that we are overlooking areas in our lives that can be used to glorify God because we have magnified our broken areas? Could it really be possible?

May I take a minute to encourage you not to sit on the sidelines all the while missing opportunities to bless others? That is one of the most beautiful things about brokenness – the realization that you can still be used by God to minister to others! What a joy!

While we are rejoicing that God can still use us in our brokenness, I want to add one word of strong caution before we move on. It's important to allow God to use the cultivated areas in your life while He is still working on the areas that need refining. If you are still trying to be freed from drugs and alcohol, it might not be wise to try to connect with another alcoholic in the beginning stages of your deliverance. The temptation might still be too great.

> *Watch and pray so that you will not fall into temptation.*
> *The spirit is willing, but the flesh is weak.*
>
> *Mark 14:38*

This is true for other struggles as well. We do not need to be perfect in an area before reaching out to someone else, but we do want to be strong enough in Christ that we pull them up and do not allow them to pull us back down.

Please don't misunderstand this to mean that we should steer clear away from ministering to others who share our struggles. That is so far from what the scripture admonishes us to do. In Luke 22:32, Peter says: *"But I have prayed for you, Simon, that your faith may not fail. And when you have turned back, strengthen your brothers."*

And just as Peter prayed for Simon, I pray for you today. Once you have turned back, strengthen your brothers (and sisters.) Having a hand up from a friend who has known our struggles and has overcome them provides an ounce of hope for someone feeling as if they are enduring their broken season in a place of loneliness and despair.

Loneliness in Brokenness

Loneliness. We've all been there. It's a place so familiar to us all that I don't have to know your name, location, or relationship status to know that loneliness is something you and I both understand.

If you happen to be there now, let me let you in on a little secret. God LOVES you! He is with you and He has not abandoned you. He is nearer to you in your brokenness than He is when you are on the mountain top. Your brokenness is a sacrifice unto Him and He is pleased with your willingness to stay in your broken place while he heals you, mends you, perfects you, and uses you. Don't flea because it is uncomfortable. Resist the urge to give up and die while you are in surgery. Hold on. He's renewing you. Giving you a new heart. Giving you life! Stay with Him and let Him do the work so that when He is done and commands you to live, you can experience the newness of His life!

The Lord is near to the broken-hearted,
and saves the contrite of spirit.

(Psalms 34:18)

Many times we miss God's closeness in our lives because we confuse God's presence with the presence of people. In other words, if we are in a lonely place and feel abandoned by people when we need them most, we tend to also feel abandoned by God. Be careful not to judge God's presence by the presence of the people in your life. God is unwavering, all knowing, and all faithful. People are uncertain, know only what you tell them, and can only support you to the extent that it does not put an additional burden and strain on their own lives. It's not that they don't love you. It's not that they don't genuinely care. It's that they are not God!

People have limitations, but our God is limitless. I believe that God is especially jealous in our season of brokenness. Deuteronomy 4:24 says: *For the LORD your God is a consuming fire, a jealous God."* If we become too dependent on people, it is possible that we will begin to give them the credit for bringing us through our rough places, restoring our lives, and bringing us into a place of healing when all the credit and glory should go to God!

We do need people and I will get to that a bit later, but anyone that God brings into our lives to help encourage us, support us, and build us up should be seen as a gift of provision from Him! Yes, we are to love and appreciate our family and friends, but we are to lean on, trust fully, depend on, and worship God and God only!

Jesus answered, "It is written: 'Worship the
LORD your God and serve him only."

Luke 4:8

Although I'd like to appear like the expert in this area, I should admit to you that I am so far from it. I am not writing this book because I have arrived and think you should hurry up and arrive, too. I am writing this book because I need you to know that there is someone right there with you totally messing up this spiritual walk, but getting up daily to try it again.

I'm getting better. But friend, let me tell you, I have had to suffer some hard things to finally gain the right perspective. Really, I guess I should say that I am *suffering* some hard things. Yes, suffering. See, this is not something I learned two seasons ago. This isn't even something I learned in the last season. Nope! This season. Learning this lesson right here in the present.

As much as I am writing to you, I am reading with you. It's personal. It's so personal in fact, that I have had to write, erase, and re-write a few paragraphs in this section several times. The sentences and phrases were well put together, but the gut wrenching truth that oozed from each paragraph made this section so difficult to write.

If I need God to do something but don't feel like it's a breakthrough I need tomorrow, I'm fine. But in those desperate and urgent situations when it seems like He is not moving fast enough, I panic. Somebody! Anybody! Help me and help me now!

In urgency, I place more dependency on a natural person than a supernatural God. Writing it in black and white makes me let out a foolish chuckle. How backwards is that?! Nevertheless, it's my truth and I had to own it before I could be free from it.

In my private introspection and prayer time, I have had to repent to God for placing people on a throne in my life that should have been His. I have had to ask for His forgiveness and then begin to release and forgive others in my life that I expected to run to my rescue in my time of crisis.

Only God can be all things to all people.

Whatever it is that you need, God can provide that and more! Practice making Him your first resort rather than your last!

Let me encourage you to take others down off His throne and put Him back where He belongs. It is when we put God back in His rightful place that we will learn that we can experience healthy, balanced relationships with others and not drain them by expecting them to be our everything – that's just too much of a burden! Place the everything burden on God and expect good people to just be good people. Allow them to love you and support you within their abilities, but only expect God to be God.

Pursuing God at all Cost

There is a woman in the Bible whose story is inspiring to me. You've probably heard of her a time or two if you just happened to grow up in church like I did. Her name is not mentioned in the Bible. Instead, it is her issue that defines her. I must admit that this has puzzled me for a very long time since it is not her issue that is talked about most, but her faith.

I know. I know. I'm jumping ahead a bit. So before I go any further, let me remind some of you of her story as I share it with some others who may not be familiar with the woman of whom we speak.

She is often referred to as "the woman with the issue of blood." She had been bleeding for twelve long years. Yep. You read that right. Twelve long years. Now, for those of you who may not be the most dedicated Bible scholars, let me take the time to tell you how lonely this woman must have been.

During this biblical period, women who had their menstrual cycles were considered unclean until after their bleeding had stopped for seven days. Anything they touched, sat on, laid on, even bathed in was also considered to be unclean. And what was unclean was to be avoided. (See Leviticus 15: 19-21)

This woman must've felt extremely isolated. She must've felt abandoned. She must've felt ashamed. And like so many of us, she had to feel broken. Broken in her body and broken in her spirit.

Her story is told three different times in the Bible and each time it is told, the story mentions how much money she spent trying to get well only to be made worse. Let me tell you. I struggled six months with an issue that doctors couldn't seem to figure out. So, believe me, I can attest that dealing with a physical issue and draining your funds trying to get well to no avail is frustrating. Extremely frustrating.

But six months would've sounded like nothing to the woman of whom we are speaking. While it was an unbearably long time to me, six months would have probably been laughable to this woman in the Bible who had exhausted her money, time, and energy for twelve long years. It's not hard to imagine that she wasn't just physically tormented, but emotionally tormented as well. I would imagine that she had to be angry, resentful, frustrated, dejected, and maybe even a little bitter.

I want us to picture her heartache and desperation. Her soaked pillow. Her anger. Her abandonment. Can you see her? Can you feel what she feels? Can you relate to her? I most certainly can. In my mind, she looks very much like me.

One day, she decided to press her way through a crowd to get to where Jesus was walking. She sacrificed being ridiculed, shamed, and banished, but she gave no concern to those things. She was so desperate for healing that she was willing to risk everything just to get to Jesus.

She pressed her way through the crowd enough just to touch the hem of Jesus' garment. Make no mistake about it. This woman wanted to see Jesus. However, when a crowd full of people made it impossible to come face to face with Him, she made a desperate move. She pressed and pressed and reached and reached until finally, she touched His clothes.

I should stop here for a minute to talk about how much faith this woman had! She didn't need to see Jesus' face. She didn't need Jesus to call her out of a crowd and prophesy to her. She didn't need a group of friends surrounding her to tell her that it was her time to be healed. All she needed was her own faith! She knew that God was powerful enough to heal her issue and her only agenda was to get close enough to touch Him! Wow!

Back to our story.

Jesus feels power leave His body and He turns and asks the crowd who it was that touched Him. The crowd around Jesus all but calls Him crazy for a few seconds. What do You mean by asking, "Who touched You?" they exclaimed. "Don't You see all these people standing around? EVERYBODY is touching You!" But Jesus knew that this was a unique touch. This was a touch of faith. The woman steps out of the crowd and tells Jesus that she was the one who touched Him.

The thing I love most about this part of the story is that the Bible says that she tells Him all. I take that to mean that she doesn't just tell Jesus that it was her that touched Him, but she also told Him why she touched Him.

If you are like me, you are probably thinking "This is Jesus!" He already knew what this woman needed. More than that, He already knew who it was that touched Him." Why then would Jesus ask who touched Him? And why would He allow this woman to tell her story to Him in front of crowds of people? Couldn't He have spared her the embarrassment?

Only Jesus can answer these questions in fullness. But do you know what I think? I don't think any of it was for Jesus' benefit at all. I think it was for the benefit of the woman and for the benefit of the crowd around her. There was a lesson to be learned from this woman's faith - a lesson about pursuing Jesus at all cost.

Jesus' acknowledgement of the woman's touch was an affirmation of her faith and an example to others that there is a reward in shaking shame, ignoring ridicule, and even ignoring reason to pursue healing.

As the woman tells Jesus her story, Jesus responds to the woman and says "Your faith has made you whole!"

I love that story! Brokenness can be beautiful, but the ultimate goal is wholeness and healing. Like the woman with the issue of blood, we must operate in faith and go after God with everything in us until He feels our touch and responds "Your faith has made you whole."

For some, this may be a quick process. Perhaps you are just starting your walk with God and have never cried out to Him before. You can know for sure that when you cry, He will answer and He will touch your broken places and bring you into healing and restoration.

For others who have experienced His healing power on a different level, He may be calling you to a higher place of faith. Don't allow this process to cause your faith to waiver. Sometimes, we can touch the hem of His garment. Other times, He wants us to seek His face.

Whatever He is calling you to do, do it! Don't stop pressing. Don't stop seeking until you find Him. It is in His presence that your joy is restored and your wounds are healed. Keep pressing until He turns and asks, "Who touched me?

And a woman was there who had been subject to bleeding for twelve years. She had suffered a great deal under the care of many doctors and had spent all she had, yet instead of getting better she grew worse. When she heard about Jesus, she came up behind him in the crowd and touched his cloak, because she thought, "If I just touch his clothes, I will be healed." Immediately her bleeding stopped and she felt in her body that she was freed from her suffering. At once Jesus realized that power had gone out from him. He turned around in the crowd and asked, "Who touched my clothes?" [31]"You see the people crowding against you," his disciples answered, "and yet you can ask, 'Who touched me?' " [32]But Jesus kept looking around to see who had done it. Then the woman, knowing what had happened to her, came and fell at his feet and, trembling with fear, told him the whole truth. He said to her, "Daughter, your faith has healed you. Go in peace and be freed from your suffering."

(Mark 5: 25-34)

CHAPTER 2

BROKEN FOCUS

We all know the saying "If you want to make God laugh, tell Him your plans!" We have probably heard it so many times that we roll our eyes the moment we hear it on the tip of someone's tongue. Yet, there is so much truth buried in that saying. God's plans are often not our plans. When we are truly yielded to His desires for our life, we may find that each time we start down our own road of success, we get a flat tire, run out of gas, or run straight off the road into a tree - and we know good and well we know how to drive a car!

Don't be alarmed. This is just a sign that God is controlling our lives and we were driving down a path that happened to be different than the one He wanted us on. Just trust the plan. The good thing about riding with God is that there is no need to worry about a blown tire or a wrecked car. He can give you a new one just like that! I mean, He's God after all!

I wish the reality of an altered path was as light hearted as a road trip gone wrong, but the truth is, oftentimes in my candid expression, it sucks!! Here we are progressing in the career of our dreams and suddenly, the company goes bankrupt and has to let us go. Or the dreams we have for our family are finally starting to come into view and all of a sudden a factor in the plan just goes awry. Maybe infertility is thrown in the picture. Maybe a spouse is diagnosed with cancer. Maybe a child moves away. All of these realities can leave us stranded on the road of life with a deflated tire, or even worse, a totally wrecked automobile.

If you have ever lost a job, had a business to fail, had a loved one to pass, experienced sickness, a divorce, a bankruptcy, a ministry failure, or any setback in life, I don't have to tell you how hard it is to be stuck in a place of disappointment and loss. I am going to beg you now. Please do not throw this book across the room or aggressively hit the exit button on your e-reader when you read this next sentence. I know that it's not an easy one to let pierce your soul when your dreams have been crushed, but it is no less true.

Brace yourself. Here it comes.

The only way to get out of that painful place is to focus on the God who is able to give you a future of restoration rather than looking at the past that you lost.

No one knows how painful those words are to absorb than I do writing this right now. I have suffered infertility, had miscarriages, and have held my breathless child in my arms. I have had financial setbacks, education setbacks, and career setbacks. Even now as I am writing these words, I am believing God for a new future with my husband who moved out of our home a few days ago and I have no idea what will happen with my marriage. Trust me. I get it.

I want to stare at that positive pregnancy test, glare at that first ultrasound, reminisce on the things I used to do when my bank account was a little fuller, dream about the love and romance my husband and I shared when all was wonderful in love and year one of marriage. And oh, do I want to keep reliving the memories I had with my precious child. Nothing would make me feel better. Or worse. Nothing would make me feel worse. Do you see where I'm going here?

Focusing on the past no matter how great or awful it seems only magnifies the past. Whether it was the best time of your life or the worst time of your life, you cannot get it back. So, if that's where your focus is, that's where you will be. Stuck. In the Past.

Now, listen. If you are reading this book, you are not allowed to stay stuck. That would defeat the purpose of the time I spent writing this, so I forbid you to stay stuck. You got it? You have to look ahead into your today. It is a requirement. I know it hurts. I know it is uncertain. I'm with you. All the way with you. You don't have to do it alone. We can do it together. But you and I, we have to look ahead into today.

I get that it would be so much easier to focus on God if there weren't people around you smiling and laughing while they are enjoying the job you lost, the family you wish you had, the home you always dreamed of and the ministry you long for. I get it. But here's the thing. They do not hold your restoration and healing in their hands. God does.

Here's another reality check for you. You're probably seeing an illusion, anyway. Sure, they probably have the happy family you long for, but you may have the financial freedom and flexible schedule they long for. They may have the career and intellect that you want, but they may wish they had the raw talent and ingenuity that you have. For a moment, consider that the smile you see on their face is because they have chosen to shift their focus from yesterday to the God who holds their today. Just a little something to ponder.

Let's get practical for a minute. I am not super spiritual. If you picked up this book thinking that somewhere in it I would tell you that you can only be saved and spirit filled if you listen to worship music 24 hours a day and keep your television on the Word Network, you have got the wrong person! I believe that God wants us to enjoy the world He created in a balanced way.

What I do believe however, is that when we are in a challenging place and have to dig in our heels to stay grounded in God's truth, it is wise to shut out some of the distractions. I am not saying that we should fast for a year and avoid anything that looks like a trigger. We would have to live in a bubble to do that.

I am however suggesting that we take some sensible steps to remove influences that may be toxic to our mindset whether they be media, entertainment, or people. Sometimes, it is necessary to change our circle so that we are surrounded by people who remind us of God's ability and sovereignty during a time where we are tempted to be bitter and turn away from Him.

Sometimes, we need to turn off shows where there is hot and heavy romance when we are single and dealing with the effects of a bad breakup. Maybe a television show highlighting fancy celebrity homes isn't the best thing for us to look at for entertainment when our home has just been foreclosed on and we have to downsize to a two-bedroom apartment.

We all have our own personal limits and only you and God know what is and is not beneficial to you in this season. As one who has had trouble conceiving, I found that initially shows that documented the lives of families bringing home their new born babies would give me hope and strengthen me to believe God for the children I desired.

Now, after experiencing miscarriages and the passing of my three-year-old daughter, those shows remind me of my losses. They are no longer good for me to watch in this season. There may come a time when these shows no longer produce an emotional trigger and are safe for me to watch again. In this season however, I have had to step back from shows like this to keep my emotions in check and my focus on Jesus.

Let's take a few moments to see what the Bible says to us about focus.

Our focus should be on things that are eternal and not temporary.

Colossians 3:2
Set your minds on things that are above, not on things that are on earth.

Our focus should be ahead of us and not on those things behind us.

Proverbs 4:25
Let your eyes look directly forward, and your gaze be straight before you.

Our focus should be on the things that advance the kingdom of God before any personal desire.

Matthew 6:33
But seek first the kingdom of God and his righteousness,
and all these things will be added to you.

There is a picture that has been circulating on the internet for a while now. I am not sure where it originated, but I have seen it at least a dozen times or more on social media. I must admit it hits me in the heart every single time I see it. The picture illustrates Jesus asking a child for her teddy bear but she does not want to let it go. The caption over the girl's head in the picture says "But I love it, God." All the while, the child does not see that Jesus has a much bigger teddy bear behind His back that He is waiting to give her.

That picture is a reminder to me that choosing to honor, serve, and obey God is always worth it! There is nothing lost or sacrificed in loving and following Christ. Even if it feels like a loss at first, the promise of

His safety, security, protection, and provision outweighs any possession that does not have His promises attached.

Sometimes, God asks us to sacrifice things that we feel are essential to our happiness and it is hard to trust Him through the process of the loss. We can be left sitting in a state of bewilderment wondering why we lost what we lost and how we could ever live again without the missing piece to our happiness.

Our focus breaks when we attempt to answer the why and how questions instead of focusing on the who and what questions. God can do more with our losses and broken pieces when we hand them over to Him than we can do with our own fragmented dreams. By remembering who is in control and what He has the power and ability to do, we can gently begin to release the pains, failures, and regrets of our past by surrendering them to Christ.

The truth is that we don't need what we think we need to be happy. We just need to remember who holds our future. When we remember this, we can let go of the job, the home, and the things we wished for our life that just didn't come to be. And we can embrace the God who holds a world of possibilities for our future.

CHAPTER 3

BROKEN VISION

I can't remember a time in life where I did not strongly feel a passion for the things of God. As my passion grew in adolescence, my mother gave me some very good advice. She said "Stephanie, you need to learn that everything in life is not spiritual!" I didn't understand it then, but boy do I understand it now!

We live in a natural world and there are some things that are just natural. God can do anything, but He will not supernaturally clean your house, mow your lawn, or make the paper work on your desk disappear. Sorry! That's just not the way it works. You must use your own physical abilities to do the task set before you!

Those may be obvious examples to some, but there are times when it really becomes hard to tell what is God and what is not. Even those that are spiritually keen sometimes miss it! If we are not careful, we can spiritualize a natural battle and naturalize a spiritual battle. The lines can blur at times and if we do not step back to examine the issue before us to determine which is which, we may end up taking actions that do not render the results we are seeking.

It is not always easy to do this when we are dealing with the things of life, especially those seasons when everything hits you at once. You know the saying, "when it rains, it pours." And sometimes, it *really* pours. And you know what? It is hard to see in pouring rain!

It is one thing to drive down a road where there is a drizzle or even mild to moderate rain. Your windshield wipers can quickly wipe away the water giving you the view of the road you need to safely navigate to your destination. But when pouring rain comes, most people either need to slow down or pull aside until the rain clears so that they safely get to where they are going.

If we are unable to see the road clearly driving in pouring rain, we are likely to drive off the road or run into a car or object and severely injure ourselves or another person. There are so many life lessons there.

Why don't we slow down when life hits us? Why don't we pull over when we need to? Why don't we ask God for help?

We could save ourselves and others if we just simply took the time to ask God for help instead of plowing along through life as if we can see. We can't see! It is pouring raining. We have no idea where we are going!

When it's blurry in our lives and we can't see, we need the guidance of the Holy Spirit to tell us how to move and when to move. We need Him to tell us when to continue straight and when to turn. These are the times when we need to pray for God's clear direction and instruction before making a move. We need to learn to ask Him for His wisdom and knowledge. And it doesn't have to be complicated.

My favorite prayers to pray are two line prayers that sound like this:

People Guidance

God, it's blurry in my life right now and I could really use some company. Is this person a good person for me to have in my life?

Business Guidance

God, it's blurry in my life right now and I am really lacking financially. Is this a good business decision for me to make?

Entertainment Guidance

God, it's blurry in my life right now and I could really use some comfort. Is this entertainment good for me to enjoy at this time in my life?

God answers the small, simple prayers just as much as He answers the long, complex prayers. I believe that it does His heart good to know that we genuinely seek His direction in our lives and that we delight in His promise to us that if we choose to steer away from our own intellect and seek Him first, He will be our guide. (See Proverbs 3:5)

Now, it's time for us to get real about the part we play in changing our lives, because as my mama used to tell me, everything in life is not spiritual! I'm going to tell you another story about a rainstorm. At my expense, it gets a little comical at the end. I'm choosing to take the embarrassment anyway, because it's a good lead into my next point.

First, I should give you a little history about how road trips work in my family. My husband drives. Always. He doesn't really like to drive, but back in his college days, he fell asleep in the backseat of a car while one of his friends was driving. They were on their way home from a spring break trip. The friend at the wheel got into a terrible accident and my husband suffered a serious arm injury as a result.

After that, I assume that my husband made some internal vow never to let anyone drive him on a road trip. Not even his wife. I understood. So, I never really pressed the issue until one day I got brave. "Hey!" I said in a jovial but serious kind of way. "We've been married for eight years. (This was three years ago.) How am I good enough to drive you around in the city but not good enough to drive you four hours away??!!! What if there's an emergency and you can't drive? How will you expect me to calmly take over if you don't ever let me drive?" My argument eventually won him over. However, he was still a little hesitant.

Now, here it is. I'm driving and feeling pretty confident thinking to myself "See! I showed him! His wife is perfectly fine at driving on road trips and he doesn't have to freak out when I'm at the wheel!" Then suddenly, at about two hours into my four-hour drive, it started to rain. I'm not going to call it a pouring storm, but the rain was coming down pretty heavily. That's the least I can give myself before I share this next part that ends embarrassingly for me.

"I can't see." I said as I turned to my husband. "It's raining really badly, and I can't see anything." I'm going to have to pull over and let you drive." My husband looked up at the windshield and down at the dashboard controls and then turned the switch. "Turn on your defogger," he said. "Oh." I said feeling pretty stupid. "Now, I can see." My husband shook his head and silently continued doing what he was doing.

I know you're probably either laughing at me or shaking your head, too. I told you it would end this way. Isn't that what we sometimes do in life though? We try to make something more spiritual than it really is. Sometimes it's not the rain blocking our vision, but the fear that we have of the rain that causes our judgement to be impaired. Everything is not a spiritual crisis. Sometimes we just need to turn a knob and keep going.

Here's another example.

A friend of mine called me on the phone one day to tell me how her neighbor was putting up new yard decorations. Some of the decorations were crossing onto my friend's side of the lawn. My friend was so stressed that her neighbor was putting these rocks on her side of the property. Yet, she hadn't said anything to her neighbor about them. When I asked my friend why she had not spoken to her neighbor, she promptly replied "I'm going to pray about it and hope that Jesus tells her to move them." I immediately replied "It's your lawn! Just go ask your neighbor to move the rocks!"

Sometimes the answer to our problems really is as simple as that. If you have an idea that may influence change, don't just pray that God will lead someone to ask you what you think. It is fine to pray for a door of opportunity. On the other hand, when opportunity arrives, don't wait for the perfect spiritual sign. Speak up!

Don't just pray that you will be tagged for that promotion when the position is open. If you know the position is open and you qualify, express your interest, and apply! You will be amazed at the opportunities we miss because we are waiting for some sort of spiritual sign that will probably never come.

Most times in our lives, our battles are a combination of both the natural and the spiritual. If you are unemployed, it is wise to ask God to carry you through this difficult season, but it is unwise to ask for manna from heaven when you are not investing in your education, cutting your own expenses where you can, and seeking new employment. Faith without your own active movement is dead. (See James 2:17)

Prayer is Always in Order

It is never out of order to pray and ask God for direction, even when dealing with a situation in the natural. Consider my friend for instance. I believe that in her situation, a prayer to ask God to go before her and create an atmosphere of peace before she approached her neighbor would've been just what Jesus desired! We should never leave God out of our decisions, but we should also never expect for Him to do what He has given us the ability to do!

Pray this prayer with me now:

God, I know that you are all knowing and all powerful! There is nothing that you are unable to do! Help me to place the tasks that I am incapable of accomplishing in my own strength into your fully capable hands. Please also give me wisdom to do the things that are within my abilities to do while always seeking to please you in my actions and in my interactions. When the lines blur, help me to take a step back and examine the situation from a balanced perspective. I know that you use the foolish things to confound the wise (See 1 Corinthians 1:27) but I never want to act foolishly out of my own mindset and call it faith. I thank You for Your wisdom, guidance, and direction. In Your Name Jesus, I pray. Amen.

SECTION 2

THE SHIFT TOWARD GRACE

CHAPTER 4

THE GRACE FACTOR

Grace is a beautiful word, but it is often misinterpreted, misperceived, and misused. Grace is not permission for us to do what we want, act how we want, say what we want and still experience the blessings of God. It is not a license to sin, but it is love and forgiveness beyond merit.

I cannot tell you how grateful I am that we have a God that is merciful and gracious enough to see beyond our failures and flaws and see our hearts. It is because of His grace that we are justified and able to stand in His presence. It is also because of His grace that we can boldly put a demand on His Word.

But it doesn't just end there.

Grace is Salvation

The grace of God is our salvation. We are not saved by our own works, but because God's grace is immeasurable enough to desire to rescue us from our sins and call us unto Himself. That is an awesome grace!

For it is by grace you have been saved, through faith—and this is not from yourselves, it is the gift of God—not by works, so that no one can boast.

(Ephesians 2:9)

Sometimes, the Christian walk will seem so challenging that it can cause us to question if we are really saved the moment we make a mistake. Rest assured that God's grace covers us! This doesn't mean that we can do as we want and act as we please. But when we let our flesh overtake us and feel the sweet conviction of the Holy Spirit, we can repent and receive the forgiveness and restoration of God.

I don't believe that there is anything wrong with making more than one public confession if we feel the need to, but when we do, we do so for the benefit of our own personal strength and walk with Christ. We really don't have to run to the altar every time we mess up and ask God to save us again. His grace has already made it so that we can repent, receive His grace, and be restored in an instant! That is an awesome truth!

I have to tell you that in my own flesh, I have issues letting go of offenses against me. I have serious trouble restoring someone who has hurt me back to their original position in my life. Usually once someone has deeply offended me, I forgive, but I keep a protective wall between myself and that other person. I'm growing in that area.

That's the beauty of God's grace and love. He doesn't keep a record of what we've done. Once He extends His grace and forgives us, He restores us back to the place in Him we were before. He's sovereign and always knows the deepest intention of your heart. He will never wall you out and there's never a reason to hide from His love.

It is Forgiveness

Can I tell you a story about a woman I know who lived in condemnation? In her heart, she desperately desired to please God, but every now and then she would mess up. She would let her anger get the best of her and say the wrong thing to a family member or friend. Or, she would slip into a negative mindset about her life for a day or two instead of focusing on God's promises and she would feel so defeated.

When this happened, she would slip further away from God because she felt like she had somehow let Him down and lost her witness. She felt like a failure as a Christian because she couldn't keep her mouth closed or her mind focused on the right things. Instead of running back to God as she should have, she sat in condemnation and defeat and beat herself up for every imperfection she found.

It wasn't until she had an encounter with God that she could change the way she saw her failures. She had to really learn that there was nothing good in her own flesh.

For I know that good itself does not dwell in me, that is, in my sinful nature. For I have the desire to do what is good, but I cannot carry it out.

(Romans 7:18)

Not one of us is perfect and that's why we desperately need the Father's grace. If we don't stay close to him, we are all in danger of falling prey to the enemy's desire for our lives.

Here's the good news. One mistake does not a failure make. The greater news is that a million mistakes does not a failure make. If we are wise enough to return to the father, admit our wrongs, and ask Him to work in us and to do for us what we cannot do for ourselves, He will forgive us and help us to rise as more than conquerors in His name.

My friend had to learn that her mistakes and weaknesses were meant to drive her to the cross and not away from it. She had to learn to shake off her self-righteous spirit and learn that anything she had ever been able to do was only because the grace of God was working within her.

This realization saved her life. It kept her chained to the cross and divorced from herself. It crucified her pride, but lifted her up in humility. And it taught her to acknowledge her humanness, repent, accept God's forgiveness, and get back up.

I hope that you are not like me. Ahem. I mean I hope you are not like my friend whose self-righteousness kept her in bondage for many years. I pray that you will choose today to learn from her experience and walk in the freedom and grace of God rather than in the pride of self.

It is Favor

A co-worker of mine has an amazing story of how she started working with the company that we both work for. In fact, it is so amazing that even when I hear her share it with someone else, I start to cry. The favor that God placed on her life in a moment when she needed it most is nothing short of amazing.

After investing over 30 years of her life working in a privately owned pharmaceutical company, she was called into a meeting and told that she had one month to find a new job. The place she had spent most of her life devoted to was closing. With one month's notice, she sought out to look for employment with the odds not in her favor. She was an older, single woman who had never been married or had any children. She had no other financial income, so her need for immediate employment was desperate.

Her age, lack of college degree, and minimal exposure to

technological developments all worked against her. It normally would have taken her months to find a job in the current market, but in just three weeks, she had found employment. Just in time! God's favor led her to the right place at the right time and she was able to start working with no lapse in her income.

I remember meeting her on her very first day at work. She smiled at each person she met, but each time she smiled, a few tears would fill her eyes. Only God could have opened the right door at the right moment for her, and she knew it!

God's grace isn't just there for when we mess up, it is there for when we need an extra measure of benevolence. He sees when we are in dire situations and because He loves us, He extends His grace to us and opens doors that would otherwise be closed.

He sees you about to spend your last twenty dollars on groceries so that your children can eat. And he moves on the heart of the person behind you to pay for the items in your cart. He sees your busy schedule and knows how quickly you need to get in and out of the bank before your next appointment. And He causes the rush to stand still for a moment. No, friends. It's not just a coincidence. It's His grace!

Grace is covering

He will cover you with his feathers, and under his wings you will find refuge; his faithfulness will be your shield and rampart.

(Psalm 91:4)

If grace could ever be described in one word, I imagine that one word would be something like "more" or "beyond." Grace is more than we deserve and beyond what we think we need. It not only allows us access to healing, restoration, and forgiveness through Christ, but it covers us and keeps us from the full recompense of our sins, bad decisions, and even words. It covers us.

It is grace that steps up to the plate when you are sitting in your car at the driver's wheel inches away from the impact of a semi-truck, and somehow your car swerves in an adjacent lane avoiding the truck and just missing the car in front of you. Total grace.

Let's be careful though. If we choose only to see the covering of grace through narrow accidents, paid bills, and shortened prison sentences, we will miss the meaning in Psalm 91:4.

Grace is not just a shield from calamity, it is a shield in calamity. His grace is our refuge and a place where we can hide in the midst of calamity. His faithfulness is a shield of grace. And when our circumstances and emotions are running rampant and seeking to tear us down, His grace is the covering we run under when we need a safe place and reprieve. It covers us.

It is Peace

This is going to sound like a dumb question, but have you ever been through a storm? I mean one of those severe storms where thunder causes the glass to shatter, the winds are howling, and it is pitch black all around? Have the storms of your life ever mirrored this? If they have, you know just what is like to feel out of control of it all. You just brace yourself for the darkness, the next gust of wind, and the next shaking and wonder how you managed to come through it all on the other side?

I am so thankful that one of the promises of God is that He will keep me in perfect peace when I keep my focus on Him. This is a promise I can rest on when I am in one of those seasons where the only answer I have is no answer. I know we've all been there. Those seasons where there are so many questions about what you are going to do next, where you are going to go next, what's going to happen next, and you just don't know.

> *You will keep in perfect peace*
> *those whose minds are steadfast,*
> *because they trust in you*
>
> *(Isaiah 26:3)*

Uncertainty without Christ is a recipe for true disaster, but when I am covered in grace, the peace of God surrounds my chaos. This is how we can walk through the storms of life, feel like we should have a nervous breakdown, but still come out in one piece.

This has been my personal testimony through every trying season. When I was hit with consecutive life shaking blows, His peace kept me.

This is not to say that I never had my times of doubt or feeling like I was absolutely about to go insane. Oh, trust me. I had them. Plenty of them. But when I pulled away from the panic and shock that flesh renders and found my secret place alone with God, He gave me His peace as a replacement for my panic. And as I felt His peace, I was able to sail through the storms of life despite the shaking, darkness, and rocky waves.

The peace of God surpassed my own comprehension and held guard over my heart and mind just as His Word promised.

> *And the peace of God, which transcends all understanding,*
> *will guard your hearts and your minds in Christ Jesus.*
>
> *(Philippians 4:7)*

One of the most meaningful examples of God's peace in my life to date happened just a few days ago. I was hit with some life altering circumstances that were out of my control but would nevertheless seriously affect me. And I happened to find out about them the night before I was scheduled to give a very important presentation at work.

I already admitted a few paragraphs ago that I tend to panic first and call Jesus second. Don't you even get judgmental with me! Some of us have learned to reverse the two, but most of us are still in the boat together. Panic first. Calm down second. Call Jesus third. Mmmhmm... I know!

Anyway, back to my story.

I panicked! In my panic, I started spiraling down a whirlwind of negative results. I knew I wouldn't be able to give this presentation. I knew that there was no one else prepared to give it. I knew that it would be very bad for me if I didn't show up at work on the day of the presentation. Very bad.

"I'm going to lose my job," I thought. "Then, I really won't be able to get through this challenge that was just placed in my lap. What in the world am I going to do?"

Yes, I know what you're thinking. And you're right. My thinking was horrible. But here's the good news. A few months ago, I would've stayed there for weeks. Maybe months. This time however, I took about an hour to have my meltdown and then decided to pull myself together.

Let that be encouragement to those of you on this journey with me. You may not put this book down, turn off the radio, or even read the scripture and suddenly be perfected in that area you are trying to grow in. It's okay. Rest assured. Little by little, with consistency and prayer, you will grow into who God has called you to be.

Okay, back to my story. Again.

When I came to my senses, I decided to call a friend, share what I was dealing with and ask them to pray for me. As they prayed, they began to ask God to make it so that I delivered my presentation at work with ease and that no one else would be able to tell that I was under intense pressure.

The following morning, I woke up and prayed that same prayer. "God, this is a bit much," I said. "But I cannot afford to let what is going on now affect the other things in my life. I have a presentation to give today, and I really, really need your help. Please help me to be so focused and energetic that others have no idea that I am under pressure."

Guess what?! He did. Not only was I focused, but I had an unusual peace even when I was surprised by unexpected upper level onlookers that would have normally made me more anxious.

The day following my presentation, multiple people came to tell me not just how well I presented, but how much they learned. This was a sign that I had done my job well – even under pressure. That's the peace of God!

And if God will do it for me, He will do it for you, too!

Let's Pray

Lord, our best efforts to please you are in vain within themselves. We need your grace to be our salvation, forgiveness, favor, and covering every moment of our lives. We have got to have you working in us and through us each and every day. Help us never to forget this truth and to seek you daily and consistently.

When we succumb to our humanity and fail in our flesh, help us to run quickly to you, admit our fallen areas, receive your forgiveness, and continue our race with your grace. In Jesus Name, Amen.

CHAPTER 5

THE FAITH FACTOR

I'm an analyst. It's what I do. Really, it's my job. It's why people hire me. I like to figure out why and how something happened. And I like to know how to fix it. This is why living a life of faith is sometimes difficult for me. Yes, I love God. Yes, I know that He loves me. But when I am walking along an unknown path and all I have to go on are His step by step directions, I tend to freak out a little bit. Maybe it's just me and that's okay. But sometimes, not knowing scares the daylights out of me. And in those moments, all I know to do is to repeat the things I just said that I know to be true. He is God. He is good. And He loves me. So, I take a deep breath. I tell my anxious feelings to be still. And I speak out four words. "God, I trust You."

This is why a few months ago when a friend asked me how I kept my faith intact through loss, setbacks, and disappointments, I wasn't quite sure how to answer her. I don't think I keep my faith at all. It's quite the opposite. My faith keeps me intact. It's the moments when I feel like I can't get through another thing, but then, somehow I look up and find that I have come through yet another trial. Those moments keep me chained to the cross. They keep me "holding on to my faith," as an old gospel song says. I know within my heart that God is real and His promises are real. This makes my faith real.

Does this mean that I don't have any doubts? No. I think phrases we tend to hear in church like "I know without a shadow of a doubt" cause those of us who sometimes feel a little shaky in our walk of faith to feel like we are falling short, but I don't think this is the case at all. We can know without a shadow of doubt that God is real, but still have doubts about how our current situation will turn out.

I heard a woman on a radio show insightfully explain this so well. "It's not that we don't trust that God will be faithful to His Word and cause all things to work for our good," she said. "Most of us believe that part. Our doubts come in when we start wondering if we will have to suffer unbearable pain in the process."

This doubt. This anxiety. This hinge of concern that we feel about our circumstances. I believe it's the very thing that makes our faith authentic. It's one thing to build our faith on the testimony of others. However, it's a completely different thing to have had and analyzed our own experiences and still come out with our faith intact. I know that this will mess with the philosophy of some of our wise walkers in the faith, but I believe a faith without a why isn't a faith at all. We should know why it is that we believe what we believe. This is how we strengthen our faith. A faith that cannot be tested and proven is a faith we wouldn't have confidence enough to share. And in this world today, we definitely need to have a faith worth sharing.

Everyone has their faith placed in something, but not everyone has their faith in God. At its very basis, faith is trust. We can trust in jobs for financial support. We can trust in a significant other for love. We can even trust in something as simple as water to quench our thirst.

Faith in one's self seems to be very prevalent in our current society. It seems that increasingly, new spiritual theologies are emerging telling us that we harness the power not to seek our God, but to be our God. I am convinced even more that as Christians, we cannot just know that we believe, we have to know why we believe. Otherwise, we might become just as lost as the people God commanded us to reach.

Things wear out and people are subject to change, but one thing is for sure. Our God is a consistent source. He will never change, never get weary, and never die out. When we make the choice to put our faith in Him, we never come up short. Now I know you may be looking at your present situation and feeling like you are a bit short. But your story isn't over. How do I know? You are alive. You are breathing. And you are able to read this book.

Even champions have moments when they feel like they will lose a game. I'm not going to tell you that they only win because they choose to keep fighting even when the game is difficult. Nope. I'm not going to tell you that at all!

Okay. So maybe I snuck it in. Whoops. Sorry for that.

What I meant to say was, even champions need a pep talk when they are down on themselves. This is usually why the coach calls a quick timeout and gives a much needed trumpet call. Or maybe he gives them a strong jolt in the pants. Hey, it's whatever works, right?

Let me be that coach in the locker room for you now. You may be down and it may feel like you're never going to get up from this one. You may feel like your faith is failing, but God is still on your side. He's never left you before and He will not leave you now.

Repeat after me. This will work out for my good and I will make it through this!! I am not just coming out of this with the victory, but I am claiming the spoils, too!

I'm waiting to hear you say it…Okay, good!

Now that we're both all pumped up and ready to fight, we can get our heads back in the game and realistically analyze our game plan.

Let's rethink this for a minute. Maybe it's not that our faith is failing us. Maybe it's really that we are failing our faith by trying to use it as a magic wand rather than a solid truth. I know. Daring thought, right? Let's examine it for a second.

What is it that we are really expecting from God? Will we choose to only believe that our faith works if this situation turns out the way that we want? Or will we choose to believe that even if this doesn't turn out how we want it to, God will bring us through it? It's a tough question to answer.

Again, I know it's a difficult reality to face. But if we are really going to come out of this book with a mindset of grace, we've got to examine our perspectives and disregard any faulty thinking that keeps us bound up in yesterday. God is not our genie. He is our father. He may not do what is easy for us, but He will do what is right for us.

Children should have faith that their parents will take care of them, provide for them, and keep them safe. Sometimes, the responsibility to provide these things means that children will not get what they want.

As much as parents want to keep their children happy, they cannot be moved by their child's temporary emotions when they make a decision that they know is best for their child in the long run. They must be firm in their guidance and direction knowing that ultimately, this decision will be for the good of their child.

When we put our faith and trust in God, we must see ourselves as His children. Because we are! He sees far down the road when we can only see the present. We must know that when we ask Him for something and trust Him to give it that He will indeed give us what we ask; it just might not look how we thought it would look.

So, if faith doesn't guarantee us our wants, why have it anyway? I'm glad you asked.

Because it pleases God

But without faith, it is impossible to please Him

Hebrews 11:6

Simply put. We should put our trust and faith in God because we love Him and want to please Him. Our relationship with God should be based on more than what He gives. It should be based on who He is. Our desire should be to know Him, worship Him, and glorify Him, not just to receive from Him.

Because It Glorifies God

"I am the LORD, that is My name; I will not give My
glory to another, Nor My praise to graven images.

Isaiah 42:8

God wants our praise, glory, and adoration to be toward Him. When we place our faith in Him to be our strength and stability during hard times, it brings glory to Him. Still, let's not make the mistake of thinking that this is for His benefit alone.

Any other person, thing, or idol that we place our faith in would be unstable. It is God who brings us through our rough places, gives us our victories, and sustains us through all of life's peaks and valleys. Glorifying Him keeps us in His presence and brings us peace. It also points others towards Him. Glorifying Him keeps us in our place of humbleness before Him. It is our recognition that we need Him every second and every moment of our lives.

Because He Can Do the Impossible

"I am the LORD, the God of all mankind.
Is anything too hard for me?

Jeremiah 32:27

God can do the impossible!! We should choose to believe Him because He is all powerful and holds our world and all creation in the palm of His hands. Never let the darkness of your circumstances overshadow what you know about God's ability to perform miracles and bring forth the impossible. Believe that God can because He is Your God!

Because it Anchors You

Our God is REAL! Our faith in Him is not simply something we cling to because we need something to believe in to get us through difficult times. It is the solid foundation that keeps us grounded at **all** times.

In a world that is constantly changing and being shaken at its very core, isn't it reassuring to know that despite what comes and what goes, what blows up and what remains, God will take care of you and keep you?! You do not have to fear because you have faith in the one thing that is sure. In life, God will sustain you, and in death, God will take you unto Himself. And that's a solid promise!

What if you are struggling to believe? What if your faith has been weakened through trials? Keep reading my friends, because your faith can be restored!

CHAPTER 6

RESTORING FAITH

James 1:3
Because you know that the testing of your faith produces perseverance

Sometimes, life has a way of knocking us so far down into a pit that we sink into a place of despair and abandon everyone and everything we thought to be secure. Yes, even the very faith that we stood on. Sometimes a simple tug towards truth gets us up and back on the right track. Other times, it takes a full on yank out of the pit to realize how far we've sunken.

Hopelessness and despair is blinding. And when we have settled into a dark place, hoping again scares the daylights out of us! After all, it's not like we never had hope. It's not like we never believed. Quite the opposite. We had hopes so high and faith so strong that we never imagined it would lead us here – sitting at the bottom of this deep, dark pit.

Oh my friend at the bottom of the pit, my heart aches for you. I know where you are. I've been there before, too.

Fortunately, I responded to the tug toward truth. But I have a few very dear friends that are still stuck at the bottom of the pit. They are so deep in that nothing short of a yank will pull them up. My heart cries for them often. I wish that they could see how much brighter it is outside of the tunnel of despair. I wish they could see how much life their place of hopelessness and despair is stealing from them. More than that, I wish they knew that the pit doesn't have to win. I wish they knew how much power they had to take their lives back. Oh, how I wish.

Maybe somebody is wishing that for you. Better yet, maybe you are wishing that for you. In that case, I am so glad that you are reading this chapter in this book at this very moment.

Listen. Satan is a trickster that wants us to believe that we can never get up once we've been knocked down, dragged down, or beaten down, but he is an outright lie! Nope, not just a liar. He is an outright lie! He has been after God's place in our lives from the very beginning; a place that was never his to claim.

Nothing makes him happier than for us to think that his lies are more powerful than God's truth. Nothing satisfies him more than when we settle for defeat instead of getting back up for the kill. He wants us to think that we are doomed for defeat so bad that he creates an illusion that keeps us from seeing that the resistance of our situation can actually strengthen our faith. Yes. You read it right. Those things that just won't give in can actually cause us to have greater faith if we make the choice not to settle for defeat.

Nothing makes a game more exciting than when the underdog makes a stunning comeback and wipes the floor with their opponent. And nothing puts more fear in the opposing team than when they've been astonishingly demolished by the team they didn't even think was a threat!

So, if life has you feeling like an underdog, it's perfectly okay. Let me scream to you way down at the bottom of that pit. It's NOT

OVER!!! And you are not out! I know you've gotten comfortable down there in the dark, but will you take one baby step of faith at a time and believe again?

Today, it can be as simple as making the choice to look up. See that small sliver of light? Just between you and me. Don't you miss it? Don't you want it again? I know believing again is scary. But I promise that there are so many more possibilities other than the one you have settled in.

You don't have to come out by yourself. You just have to want out and reach out. It's that simple.

Faith by Circle

Have you ever been convinced of something just because so many people said it? I had this experience recently and let me tell you, it was no laughing matter. Well…maybe it was a small one.

I like to use my breaks at work to get my exercise in for the day. So, I walk around the perimeter of our office building once in the morning and once in the afternoon. A co-worker noticed me walking one day, and said, "Be careful! We have snakes out there and they are the kind that chase you!" Now, she wasn't intentionally trying to scare me, but I did have a mini panic attack. For one, I never knew that snakes were fast enough to chase! And for two, I am a girly girl and very much afraid of slithering reptiles! But, when I calmed down, I rationalized that this was just one person and no one else had said anything of the sort. I also hadn't seen any snakes with my own eyes, so… Hakuna Matata, right?

In case you've been sleeping under a rock for the last twenty years, Hakuna Matata is a saying from my favorite Disney movie *The Lion King*. It means "no worries."

Now, back to things of importance.

A few weeks passed and I happened to run into another co-worker who happened to have her son with her. "Be careful," the co-worker's son said. "We were walking around the other day and we kept finding snakes everywhere."

"Wow! It must be true." I thought to myself. "I have really got to start watching out for snakes." And watch, I did. Every single time I passed a bush and saw anything shaped like an "s" or something that resembled a reptilian tail, I jumped. Every single time! And to this day, I have yet to see an actual snake! But I believe that they are out there.

Just the same, when I am believing for God to do something in my life that I haven't yet seen, my faith is encouraged and built up even more by hearing the testimonies of others. This is one of the reasons Hebrews 10:25 encourages us not to forsake the assembling of ourselves together, but to exhort each other all the more. When we come together and share our testimonies, we build each other's faith.

Trust me. You are not the only one who has been through the fire and felt like you came out smelling like smoke and tar. Someone else's testimony will strengthen you through your test. Find someone else who has been through or made it through. And let them encourage you.

They triumphed over him by the blood of the Lamb and
by the word of their testimony; they did not love their lives
so much as to shrink from death. Revelation 12:11

Faith by the Word of God

I have to admit something to you here. I have been one of those people that had the tendency to fall off the wagon when it came to reading my Bible. Sure, I read it a few times a week. And yes, I did pick it up outside of church. But after life picked me up, put me in its mouth, chewed me up, and threw me up, let me tell you, I had my Bible open at all times of the day and the night.

I have since learned that the level of faith I exhibited in difficulty was directly correlated to the amount of time I spent each day allowing the Word of God to penetrate my spirit. When I am built up on His promises, I don't let a little trial throw me off because I know that He will direct each step that I take if I seek His will. (See Proverbs 3:6) When I am not full of His Word, I tend to think that I have to be in control of my trials. And this causes me to spin completely out of control.

If you are struggling to believe God for a positive outcome in the midst of your difficulty, start filling yourself up with His promises. I guarantee you that you will be encouraged to trust Him again!!

Faith by Speaking

After you have committed yourself to meditating on the Word of God, commit yourself to begin speaking those promises and words of faith out of your mouth. Life and death live in the power of the things that you speak (See Proverbs 18:21) so open your mouth and begin to use your faith to declare what the Word says about your life. If you don't know how to start this, keep reading. There's an exercise in Chapter 8 that will help jumpstart your faith declarations.

When we are declaring a thing and even calling a thing forth, we need to be sure that it lines up with the Word of God. I have heard many people use their faith for something outside of God's will and then feel like God let them down when it somehow does not work out that way. Remember that God is bound by His Word, not ours.

When we know that we are praying and speaking in a way that

lines up with God's promises and will for our lives, we can be bold in our declarations knowing that we have the Word of God backing us up!

A prayer that God will strengthen your faith:

Father, I pray that the person reading this right now is renewed in faith even through times of testing and trial. I pray that you would surround them with others who are standing on Your Word and know just how sure your promises are. Father as they mediate on Your Word, show them Your promises and will for their life. Help them to begin to stand strong and speak those things until they see change. Thank you for strengthening and renewing their faith right now! In Your Mighty Name. Amen.

CHAPTER 7

GRACE IN A SHATTERED PLACE

There is nothing more painful than the moment God answers your prayer, but it seems like He hasn't answered at all. You prayed for healing and sickness remained. You prayed for a relationship to be restored, but then someone in the relationship decides to sever ties. You prayed for financial increase, but you lost your job instead. You prayed for children, but instead you hopelessly endured costly fertility treatments to no avail. You prayed for a loved one to be healed of cancer, but instead, they passed away. It seems as if God didn't hear you at all. And if he did, it sure seems like he has you on the list of people that He just doesn't like.

Let this Chapter be your encouragement. God did hear you and He did answer you. Although it may not seem like it now, His answer was something more beautiful than the change you prayed for, it was grace. The change you desired may have satisfied your fleshly craving, but God's flowing grace in the shattered places of our lives is what really heals us, fulfills us, and satisfies our souls.

I will never forget the day I received the phone call that no parent ever wants to receive. I was sitting at my desk at work and the words on the other end of the phone ripped my heart out. "Yes ma'am. We are calling because we went to wake your child up from her nap and she is not responding and not breathing." I remember jumping up from the chair, rushing to my boss' office to tell her I had an emergency and driving to my daughter's daycare just three minutes away. I got to the daycare and barely parked my car in a parking space. The paramedics were bringing my daughter out on a gurney as I jumped out of my car.

I tried to keep my emotions under control as I walked up to the ambulance. "Can I see her?" I asked. The paramedic asked me who I was. "I'm her mother." I responded abruptly. "Well ma'am," the paramedic said. "You can see her for a minute, but she has no pulse and she is not breathing."

I will remember these next moments for the rest of my life. They barely let me peek at my daughter and touch her hand before they closed the door. I jumped into the front of the ambulance all the while looking at the paramedics trying to resuscitate her through the ambulance window. I began to do what I knew to do and pray. "God." I cried. "You are a healer and I need You to heal my daughter."

We arrived at the hospital after what seemed to be an eternity. The doctors attempted several times to get my daughter's heart to beat, but they were unsuccessful. They came to me as if they were talking about some baby doll that had been lost on an amusement park ride. "She's gone." One of the doctors said as she touched me with her very cold hands. I will never, ever forget that moment.

I picked my daughter up expecting to feel her legs and arms wrap around me. Instead, her body was cold and limp. Nothing could have ever prepared me for that experience. Nothing.

The days immediately after were sort of a blur. It's hard to think straight when your child just doesn't come home one day and all of a sudden you have to figure out how to live the rest of your life without the child who brought so much joy and love into your life.

A few weeks after her memorial service, the reality began to set in and I was faced with a choice. I could rightfully be angry with God and walk away from Him. Or I could choose to trust that He loved me despite what my circumstances were telling me. I could choose to never pray again because He didn't answer this prayer as I had wanted. Or I could trust that His answer was in giving my daughter a permanent healing.

Although full of life and energy, my daughter was born into this world with an abnormal heart. She was strong. Strong enough to make it through three heart surgeries prior to being six months old. Looking back, I can now see how it may have been for her good that she got to live with Jesus rather than having to undergo continuous surgeries as a small child. Still, that's not an easy resolution for a mother to come to. It's not an easy one for a father to come to, either.

I had to trust God even though He didn't answer my prayer like I thought He should. I had to choose to believe that He would carry me through the pain and darkness and give me new hope.

The dark days were very dark and the pain seemed unbearable most times. In fact, I have had to stop writing this to regroup several times because the memory of it all is still so very painful. There is only one way I could have ever made it through and that is by the very grace of God.

Grace is that thing that helps us to endure pain when we think it will take us out. It keeps us when we want to fall apart and it holds us when we want to let go. I remember driving home some days fantasizing about driving my car into a tree. Thank goodness the grace of God kept me!

Grace is different than miraculous change. It doesn't give us the easy way out, but it does make the way out easy. It doesn't remove the pain, but it does help us endure the pain. It doesn't give us the answer; it leads us to the answer.

God doesn't always give us change. Sometimes, He gives us grace and allows us to walk through the situations we wanted Him to change. Peter prayed for God to remove the thorn from his flesh three times. God did not remove the thorn. Instead, He said to Peter what He said to me when my daughter laid breathless on that hospital table. He said to Peter what He is saying to you through your trial now, "My grace is sufficient."

But he said to me, "My grace is sufficient for you, for my power is made perfect in weakness." Therefore I will boast all the more gladly about my weaknesses, so that Christ's power may rest on me.

(2 Corinthians 12:9)

We all have thorns. They may be habits, attitudes, painful situations, or trauma filled backgrounds. Whatever the thorn, know that God's grace is sufficient because it keeps us reliant upon Him.

To be our Help

If you are a parent that is either currently experiencing or that has previously experienced the independence of the toddler stage, you know how frustrating it can be when your child is trying to put on their shoes and keeps putting them on the wrong feet. They will have emotional breakdowns and tantrums when they can't figure it out themselves, but they will not let you help! Of course, it is always much more frustrating when you are running late and trying to get out the door. You know that you can do it much faster and much better than they can, but they continue to fight for their independence. Because, well… they can do it!

If we are good parents, we give our children independent task to do as we know that they are able to handle them, but for the tasks that may still be a little difficult, we need to help them and they need to allow us to help even though, well... they can do it!

It's the same thing with God, friends! We could probably figure this complex issue out ourselves, but the twist and turns and knots we encounter along the way can be much worse if we do not rely on God's grace and allow Him to be our help. He has seen the road ahead and has already been there. He knows how many circles it will take and how to tell which way is right and which way is left.

To be our Strength

There are moments when we will feel that we are not strong enough to carry the load that we have and that is when we need the grace of God to come in and be our strength. God's Word tells us that His strength is made perfect in our weakness. This means that God works best when we are weak and feel like we can't take another step or go another mile.

Recently, I talked with a Christian counselor about the load I am currently having to bear. I was just about down to tears and began to continuously say "I just can't do this." "You're right." The counselor said. "You can't do it."

Well, put a fork in me. I'm done for sure. You don't really expect the counselor to agree with your desperation. "*You* can't do it," he continued. "But **God** through you can." That was the reminder I needed to know that the battle I was currently facing was not my battle, but God's.

So many times, we come against a problem and we throw at it all we've got. It's no wonder we get burned out, overly stressed, and emotionally depleted. Remember that we have to determine what type of battle we are facing and resolve not to naturalize a spiritual battle.

There are some battles we need to learn to rest through and let God's grace and strength fight on our behalf.

To be Our Comfort

Wouldn't it be lovely if all of our family members and friends understood life exactly as it happened to us? Wouldn't it be nice if they understood desperation the way we felt it when we felt it? After all, if they could feel what we felt they would likely be able to comfort and coddle us just the way we wanted them to, right?

Perhaps that's why God didn't leave us here as spirit only, but as flesh. We have our own thoughts, feelings, and emotions. And yes, we all have our own problems. We are all dealing with one thing or another and sometimes our own problems keep us from being a comfort to our friends and family.

I don't know the mind of God. But I can almost imagine that in His perfect design, this is exactly how He wanted it. He longs to be our rock. He longs to be the One we run to in times of discomfort and trouble just as a parent longs to be the arms of comfort for their own child. He wants to show us how much He loves us and is for us. He wants us to know the sweet comfort of His touch. That's the kind of Father we have.

We're not always the kind of children that know the depth of our Father's love, though. We usually run from here and there and from person to person. We are always trying to find someone that will say the right words or embrace us with just the right amount of pressure for the exact amount of time to make what we're feeling go away. So, we try friend after friend and lover after lover. Sometimes, we even try thing after thing seeking to find that comfort that can only be found in the arms of Jesus.

Oh, if we would go to our Father, tell Him where it hurts, and run into

His arms. He will kiss away our tears, whisper words of encouragement in our ears, rock us through the night, and help us to get back up and fight. His comfort is there for our dark places. It is there for our weaknesses. It is there for our failures. And it is there for every loss we face. If we would only learn to trust Him to be our comfort, we would find that healing everlasting flows from the very nature of God who is our Father.

To Be Our Hope

Our Father! That's exactly who Daddy God is. And just like a father who wipes away our tears, He helps us to get up from our pain and press forward into the newness of tomorrow. Pressing on isn't an easy feat after going through storm after storm after storm, but because God is our hope, we can press on knowing that yesterday's storms give way to tomorrow's rainbows.

Wait. That was a cliché. I know I promised I would limit those. Hopefully though, we've come far enough on our journey together that you trust that I understand your struggle. Maybe we've even come far enough that we can… redefine the word rainbow??

For I know the plans I have for you," declares the Lord, "plans to prosper you and not to harm you, plans to give you hope and a future.

(Jeremiah 29:11)

I hesitated to use this scripture because it is one so frequently quoted that I just assume we all know what it means, and therefore, we all understand the promise. Maybe those of us who quote it do know what it means. Maybe we even understand the promise. But, I chose to use it for the newcomer in Christ who may have never come across this reassuring Bible promise.

And... I chose to use it for the Christian reading this who is just like me. They know that God has a plan for them. They know the scripture. They recite the scripture. They even share the scripture with others. But, they still forget its promise sometimes when they are in the trenches.

I had a moment like this just before I starting writing this book. Yes, me. The person writing these words to you right now. I had a moment of despair and I forgot all about those Bible promises that give hope and encouragement in the midst of struggle.

I was tired of enduring storm after storm and felt like I had nothing left. So, I went down to my local wholesale store, purchased a large bottle of pills and checked myself into a hotel. I remember that day vividly. My mind tossed back and forth between fighting with tenacity and giving up instantly. I was a mess.

I wouldn't talk to relatives, friends, or church members because I didn't want to hear that God had a plan and that I needed to trust Him. I wasn't angry at God. I was just tired! I decided that with or without Him, I had enough of enduring seasons filled with insurmountable pain. I was worn out. I was weak. I didn't see a way out of this storm. I didn't want to see a way out. I just couldn't do it.

So in a hotel room all by myself, I looked at a bottle of pills one minute and cried uncontrollably the next. If I could've promised myself with certainty that those pills would've given me peace, I would've taken them. But I knew better than that.

I knew that most suicide attempts were not successful. And usually, they render an already depressed or suffering person more suffering and depression from newly created medical problems.

More than that, I knew that God's plan for my life would supersede my own. If God wanted me to live, I would live. It's possible that I would've lived with a damaged liver and a shorter lifespan than planned, but I would live. Because I am not in control. God is.

It was at that moment that I remembered Jeremiah 29:11. God's plans are to bring me to a future of hope and an expected end. Can I be honest? I don't know what my end will be. I don't even know what the end of that storm will be. While I wish I was writing from the other side of the storm, I am actually writing through it. What I know for sure is that on the other side there is hope and an expected end.

Friend, will you take my hand and come out of the dark shadows of despair? I know what it's like to be there. I was there a short time ago, but in God, we have hope. We have hope that our darkest storms will bring something good to fruition.

Our broken dreams can be restored or they can birth a new dream. Our broken homes can be put back together or they can cause us to pursue a new level of wholeness. Our failing health can bring healing or cause us to be a light for others during pain. Whatever our despair, God can be our Hope!

A note from my heart:

> In writing the above section, I had to stop and take a moment to address the loved ones of those who have left this earth by way of suicide. Please know that by sharing my own personal story of healing, I am not saying that God wanted me to live any more than He wanted your precious, precious children, parents, relatives, and friends to be here. I don't have answers for suicide just like I don't have answers for homicide. Please know that God's love is just as real for you and your loved one as it is for me. As you continue to read this book, maybe even with a knot in your heart, know that God's love reaches you in the very place that you hurt.

CHAPTER 8

EMBRACING GRACE

Listen, you do not need to spend one more minute crying your eyes out about how your life has turned out up until now, what dreams haven't come to pass, and what things you have lost. You just do not have that much time! Your time is precious. And beyond that, your heart has been aching so long that it is screaming from the pain! Your heart needs you to get up!!!

From Depression

Just a few days ago, I sat in my living room with a close friend and began to share with her a moment from the days immediately following the death of my daughter. I remember laying in the bed for days at a time. I only got up to use the bathroom and maybe to eat. I spent most of my time mindlessly playing a computer game all day while crying. I laid in my bed so long that my body ached. It was by far the darkest season of my life. In just writing those few words, I get vivid memories of that time. It was dark.

I know what it is to not be able to see the sunshine even when it is bright around you. It's a miserable place and believe me, it is more painful than any physical pain I have ever felt. But that's why I had to get up. And so do you.

I don't think anything pulls a person down stronger than depression. Depression is an ugly, dingy, dark cloud that sits over you, drains your energy, messes with your perspective and steals your life. Once it has gotten a real hold on you, it's really hard to find the way out. But don't be discouraged. There is a way out.

I want to be careful and sensitive as I write this next part of the book. I am writing as someone who has dealt with depression from a spiritual and situational aspect, but I am aware that depression is also a clinical condition. I believe in supernatural deliverance, but sometimes deliverance is a process that we must walk out in the natural.

Don't sit in your dark room of silence afraid to reach out for help. Nor should you allow anyone to convince you that you are not strong or do not have enough faith if you are unable to beat depression through prayer and positive thinking alone. Get up and get to a professional now!

There is too much purpose in you for you to die in this place! Do not let the enemy destroy you because you are afraid to get help or afraid of what others might think. Follow the leading of the Holy Spirit and the sound medical advice of trained professionals.

Okay. Now that I have that out of the way, let's spend some time talking about how God can help us to get up from the depression that comes from hope deferred and a down-trodden spirit.

Step 1 – Tell God

Many times when we are down-trodden and depressed, we feel that God somehow let us down. We prayed for something, believed that God would do it for us, and felt let down when it didn't happen.

When we experience those heartaches, our whole world can seem as if it is crashing down and falling apart. If we are not honest with God about how we feel, it can leave us bitter and cause us to drift away from God in the moments we should pull closest to Him.

Don't be afraid to tell Him what's in your heart. He can handle it. He is big enough to handle your frustrations and disappointments and longs for you to draw close to Him even when you are hurting. That's the first step towards walking into your healing.

For we do not have a high priest who is unable to empathize with our weaknesses, but we have one who has been tempted in every way, just as we are--yet he did not sin.

Hebrews 4:15

Step 2 – Tell a friend

People are important – especially when you are feeling depressed, overwhelmed by life, or stuck in a pit. You need people. But, let me be very clear. You need safe, spiritually mature people that will edify you, uplift you, and then point you to Jesus. The kind of people surrounding you are important when you are low emotionally because you want to make sure your circle of friends helps you up and does not encourage you to stay down.

Many times, we feel that we are rightfully bitter in our own human nature. But bitterness that continues to fester under the surface never leads to healing. And bitterness that festers on the inside will eventually show up on the outside.

Your friends should allow you to be honest, but they should also encourage you to press forward. Sometimes, God will send you a circle of friends like this, but more often than not, He sends you one or two people. Remember, this is the season of your life where He wants your attention to be on Him more than anything or anybody else.

Step 3 – Release it at the altar

Okay, you told God. You told a friend. What's next?

Let it go.

Build an altar in your heart and give that thing to God, the only One who can do something about it. If you continue to carry it, it will burden you down and you will never be able to move beyond whatever your "it" is. So, do yourself a favor and let it go!

Let's practice now by saying this prayer:

God, I have told you all about my disappointment over (speak your disappointment here.) I have also shared my disappointment with a friend in order to empty the contents of my heart. Now, I lay this disappointment at your feet. I know that I cannot go back and change it, but You can somehow use it to make me better and give me a better future. Take this burden of heaviness and give me a garment of praise. I release this weight of disappointment and embrace the lightness of your peace and contentment. In Your Son Jesus' Name, Amen.

Step 4 – Praise

Let me tell you, true praise is a weapon and it will cause you to see things differently. Nothing sends the enemy running like a praise!!! Did you just start praising Him like I did?

Most times we fail to activate the power of praise in our lives because we get it all wrong. We tend to think praise is about a song, a shout, or a hand raise, but we are so amiss! Praise is about magnifying God! The online dictionary says that the word "magnify" means to make greater in actual size or to enlarge. There is another definition that says to magnify means to make "more exciting." I love that one!

Life is full of drama. And drama can be exciting! When it's not happening in our own lives, it is what draws us to the movie screen just waiting to see what is going to happen next. We glue ourselves to the screen waiting to see what the next plot twist will be.

When we choose to magnify God, we are choosing to put faith in His plan, watching and waiting to see what will happen next. God is so much more awesome and so much more exciting than whatever the drama, whatever the problem, and whatever the issue is in your life. Even if you can't predict how your current situation will end now, you can know with certainty that God is not going to disappoint you!

Reflection:

Are you going through the motions or are you really magnifying God? I challenge you to become more excited about His ability than your current problem and then sit back and watch Him work!

From Defeat

This would be a really good time for a sports analogy, but I don't have one, so please forgive me for that. I was not given a single athletic talent and I don't care much for watching sports on television either. I watch Football and Basketball from time to time, but not enough to provide an analogy that real sports fanatics would appreciate. I will just have to go to with what I do know well. Music.

While there are so many good things about modern technology and the ability to record and instantly replay live experiences, I can't help but feel sorry for music performers today. If you happen to be a singer, musician, Broadway actor, or something of the sort, I can imagine you know what I mean. Everybody has an off day. Everybody. Maybe the sound is off. Our voice isn't quite right. We can't hear the people on stage with us. So many factors.

Recently, one of my favorite singers had to have at least one of these factors happen to them as they performed at a live Christmas event. Oh, the time the masses had with their performance as videos traveled across the internet faster than it took some of us to type a single sentence. "That was awful!" some of the comments said. "Were they high?" I read as another comment came in. And yes, although I made no written comment, I too, wondered what made this usually flawless and glorious sounding vocalist give a performance that was not so flawless and glorious.

Just a few weeks after this video traveled the world via the World Wide Web, this same artist delivered a stunning vocal performance in another setting. If you placed the videos up against each other, turned your head away from the images and simply listened, you probably wouldn't even know they were performances given by the same artist.

Here's the statement that second performance made. One bad show does not define me as an artist.

Our lives, when lived well, should make the same statement. One shattered dream does not mean my life is shattered. One failed venture does not mean that I am a failure. One broken relationship does not mean that all my relationships will be broken.

Somehow, as we move through life and experience more failures and heartaches, those words just don't ring as true for us. Sure, a singer that has already made a name for themselves can get back up and give a stellar performance. But it takes years to recover from bankruptcy after a failed business venture. It takes counseling and time alone to heal after a failed relationship. It takes therapy, medicinal treatments, surgery, and sometimes even the acceptance of a new way of life after a heart wrenching medical diagnosis.

All of this is true. But here's the truth that we miss when our focus is set on our failure alone. We are still here and our story isn't over. We have the ability to get up and try again, sing again, dance again, play again, build a business again, write again, even love again. We can get up from failure.

From Damaging Thoughts

Our thoughts play a huge part in our capacity to stay down or bounce back. If our thoughts are depressing, we will be depressed. If our thoughts are joyful, we will be joyful. The truth is simple, but the process is not. It is not easy to think joyful thoughts when our lives have been turned upside down and all around. It's not easy when we have no idea what is happening, how to stop it, or whether or not we should walk, run, jump, or stand still. It is not easy to think peaceful thoughts when our lives are full of chaos, but it is possible. And the quality of our lives depends on us choosing to make the switch.

So, how do we make the switch? I am glad you asked. The Bible instructs us to think on those things that are noble, lovely, true, and of good report. That's the prescription for joy and peace. If we have trouble in our life, there is often still something good no matter how small, and that is a good place to start!

Finally, brothers and sisters, whatever is true, whatever is noble, whatever is right, whatever is pure, whatever is lovely, whatever is admirable–if anything is excellent or praiseworthy–think about such things.

(Philippians 4:8)

Indulge me for a moment and complete this exercise with me. Take out a sheet of paper and fold it in half. On one half, write down every negative thought you can think of about your life, yourself, and where you are right now. Be very honest with yourself about the thoughts that you are thinking. You cannot combat them if you do not acknowledge them. On the opposite half of the paper, write down a truth that refutes the thought you wrote on the other half. For this part of the exercise, I want you to only focus on personal truths. We will get to Biblical truths shortly.

Example:

Negative Thought	Personal Truth
I feel unloved	I have friends and family that love me and pray for me on a consistent basis
I feel alone in my struggle	I don't have many people around me, but I do have one close friend who is walking with me through this trial
I don't feel valuable	I have a unique personality and unique gifts and talents that I can share with others. This means that I have value.

Now, take that same sheet of paper and tear it along the fold. I want you to look at the side of the paper where you wrote all your negative thoughts. Is there a theme to some of the things that you are thinking?

In my example above, I can see a theme of feeling unloved, alone, and insecure.

Really examine and write down any themes you notice in your thoughts. Then, write them down on a separate sheet of paper. Now, take some time to search the Bible to see what God's Word says about the thoughts that are running through your head.

Example:

I feel unloved

God's Word Says: God's love for me is everlasting

Jehovah appeared of old unto me, saying, Yea, I have loved thee with an everlasting love: therefore with lovingkindness have I drawn thee. Jeremiah 31: 3

I feel lonely

God's Word Says: God is always with me.

Be strong and courageous. Do not be afraid or terrified because of them, for the LORD your God goes with you; he will never leave you nor forsake you." Deuteronomy 31:6

I feel inadequate

God's Word Says: I am more than capable.

I can do all things through him who strengthens me. Philippians 4: 13

Once you have addressed all of your negative thoughts with God's Word and a personal positive truth, take that piece of paper with all of the devil's negative lies and throw it in the trash where it belongs!!

Take your newfound positive truths and life breathing scriptures and post them somewhere where you will see them frequently. Make it your task to go to them and say them out loud when those negative thoughts try to come back and take root in your mind. Remember that you have thrown them in the trash and replaced them with the truth!

From Downgraded Dreams

My favorite book of the Bible is probably one that may be the least favorite to others because no one really wants to experience what this man in the Bible did. I am talking about my man, Job. Job lost everything, and I do mean everything – wealth, health, family, friendship, and love. It's quite a depressing story if you stop in the middle. But the middle is not my favorite part of the story. Let's be real. The middle isn't really anyone's favorite part of a story. The middle is where all the mess happens. But the story would never be quite as good without the mess. Anyway, I digress…

Job started off as a rich man and had favor with God. It would be easy to fall in love with the beginning of his story, but that's not where my love affair begins either. It's the very end! Four little words at the end of the book to be exact - **after this, Job lived!!**

Those powerful words have stuck with me through the hardest times in my life. It is a reminder to me that God will always upgrade you!

Job was a rich man. He had a nice house, fine cattle, a wonderful family, and good friends. God allowed the enemy to wreak havoc in his life and take everything he had, just to see if Job would still remain faithful to God.

This story is a reminder to many of us that even though God does not cause our troubles, He does allow some things into our lives to test our faithfulness. We should remember in those times that God is still protecting us. God gave the enemy permission to touch everything around Job, even his body. But God would not allow the enemy to touch Job's soul. Just like in Job's life, God is in control of the storm and the test in your life and He will only let the devil go so far. Don't allow your heart to drift from God when it seems He has forsaken you. He's got your back! Just keep holding on!

When the test was over, Job received double what he lost! Double!! And his years were full!

God has not changed. His power has not weakened and He has not run out of things to restore in your life! Stop thinking that because plan A didn't work that you should fall back on a much smaller plan B. No, no, no. That is not the restoration mindset. Think bigger. Think Plan A+! Dust off your dreams and go bigger! Think double. Think like you thought you would be living then, but now, you are really going to live. Don't go through a Job experience without getting a Job victory!!!

Get up and upgrade your dream!!

CHAPTER 9

AN UNFAILING GOD

Alright friends, listen closely. People are human and they will fail you. No qualms about it. They will be busy when you need them most and forget when you need them to remember. They will have a bad day when you need them to cheer you up and they will be tending to their own health when you, too, are sick. They just will!! And most likely, it won't be because they don't love you.

It will be because they have their own lives and own plans. They forget things. They get stressed. They get sick. They have bills, too. They are human. I know we've covered the people will be people part a while back in a previous chapter, but it bears repeating.

And yes, it does make a really good intro into this chapter, but that's not the point. Trust me. You need to read this again. I need to read this again. Our friends need to read this again. We all need to be reminded that the people we love and the people that love us are just people. And because they are people, they will at some point in our lives undoubtedly fail us. That's just the way life is. The only One who will not fail us is God.

Say this with me. God alone is unfailing. Say it again. God ALONE is unfailing. Let it sink way down to those childhood hurts and rejections. Let it flow to those word wounds by your family and those disappointments left by unmet expectations. God alone is unfailing. Your parents are not God. Your children are not God. Your spouse is not God. Your friends are not God. Your church is not God. God alone is unfailing. And only God can be God. Got it? Good.

Now, here's the good news. Ready? GOD is unfailing. He won't fail you on a special day. He won't fail you on an awful day. He won't fail you on a needy day. He will be there. He will listen. He will comfort. He will provide. And He will guide.

In one of the worst seasons of my life, I remember feeling so frustrated with people. It was obvious that I was overwhelmed. I mean obvious. I was drowning in despair after I had been hit with yet another family tragedy and I had no energy to do this one foot in front of the other thing.

I was desperate. So, I did something I don't usually do. I screamed for help! But the response I got back was painful as many people only offered sympathy and said that they would pray for me. I felt like I was breaking, and yet, I felt even more alone.

Don't get me wrong. I think prayer is the most powerful weapon on earth. But when I am drowning and in water so deep that I take a step and do something so unusual as to share my pain, I hope that in return someone is at least available to stand by me and help me get back up on my feet. But instead, they told me they would pray for me.

I can't tell you how many ways I struggled with this response and on how many levels. Not only did I feel alone, but I also felt exposed and embarrassed. And these feelings led me down into a deep pit. And that's just where the devil wanted me to stay. Deep in anger. Deep in resentment. Deep in negativity. Deep in rejection.

The deeper I sunk, the happier he got. The more I assigned negative thoughts to others, the more I isolated myself from them. And the more I isolated myself, the more access the enemy had to my mind.

"You're foolish." The enemy would say. "You just shared a humiliating piece of your life with people you thought you could trust and where are you now? Still alone. Still humiliated. And now to add, you're embarrassed."

I didn't realize it at the time, but there was a root of bitterness in my heart that planted itself at the very first thought. And with every negative thought afterwards, bitterness grew and grew.

Then, one Sunday afternoon, I decided to listen in to a sermon online that gave me the wake-up call I needed. "How often do we miss the small miracles God does in our life thinking about all of the things and people we wanted Him to send that He didn't send?" The well-known preacher seemingly shouted directly at me through my tablet. I sat on my bed while listening to this message and cried. And I mean cried. Maybe bawled is a more appropriate word. Yes, bawled. That's what I did.

I was going through a storm, but there were so many ways that God provided in the midst of the storm that I hadn't been grateful for at all. I was angry that I was in a storm and that people didn't show up for me like I wanted them to show up. I was angry at the storm. And I was ungrateful for the miracles in the midst of the storm. I repented.

I wanted people, but I needed God. There was no way that any person or group of people could be what I needed in my storm. They had their own lives. They had their own problems. But God was big enough to handle my storm and theirs, too.

They were wise in their response to me. Although it felt like a harsh response at the time, here's what they were actually saying. That list of needs you have right now. There's no way I can fill it and there's no way I'm going to even try to. You need God. I care about you so much that

I'm not going to step in and try to be a piece of what you need when God can be all that you need, so I am going to send God.

And God was there. He walked me through every piece of the storm and held me together when I had already fallen apart. Delightedly, God mends things that are broken. So, he picked up every broken piece and gently began the mending process of my life while I was going through the storm.

Please, don't get me wrong. We do need people to be there for us, to love us and encourage us. And sending God when we could possibly be the answer He sends is not the solution either. We all need to work with God for the good of each other. We all need to recognize our healthy need for people and community and we all need to be the kind of people and community that someone else needs.

But, there are needs in our lives that only GOD can fill! And we need to learn to recognize those God needs and know that He is able to fill them in ways we couldn't possibly hope for or imagine.

During my difficult season, I couldn't even communicate an effective need because I was so broken. I didn't see it then, but in the process of healing, I started to walk through the beginning stages of balanced need and dependency on people and it sounded much different than my initial cries for help.

Initially, I could only communicate that I needed help. I left others to identify and determine what that help meant. As I healed, I began to name it. I need to go to lunch. I need to talk. I need you to listen without offering advice. These were needs that people could understand without playing the guessing game. And they also weren't so overwhelming that others felt like they had to be God to meet them.

I started getting more people willing to step in and help than sympathy and prayer responses simply because I was no longer making an unrealistic request for some human person to come in and do God's job in my life.

As I started to reflect on my own unreasonable expectations for people to meet God needs in my life, I came to a few conclusions about why I had this expectation and why others do, too. At the basis, we expect this type of treatment because it's what we would give to others. But why are we so willing to swoop in and play the rescuer for others? Let's talk about it.

Reason One: We have our own God complex

Yes, I said it. A God complex. We may not intend for this to be our reality. But when we take on the load of others as to try to prevent them from feeling hardship, pain, or reap the benefits of their own decisions, we are playing God. The Bible does say we are to bear each other's burdens, but the word bear means to uphold and support. Not to carry. If I am supporting someone in their trouble, I am there for them to lean on or a shoulder for them to cry on, but I do not see myself as the fixer of their problems. I cannot be their problem fixer. I am not their God.

Hear me parents of grown-up children. You can plant seeds and encourage your children to follow the right path, but you cannot live their life for them. Although you can try to rescue them from the consequences of their decisions, I can always guarantee you it will end up costing you more than you imagined. When there are no consequences, there is very little reason to keep that same decision from being made again. Furthermore, being a rescuer might very well rob you of the years you are meant to enjoy living your own life. I know it pains you to watch those you love travel down difficult paths, but you cannot be their God.

Reason Two: We hate to see others in pain

In itself, this is a beautiful sentiment. We are moved with compassion when others are in pain and we want to do what we can to absolve their pain. This is the heart of Christ. So, should we stop feeling this way all together? I happen to think that the answer is not in throwing this sentiment away all together, but walking in balance.

When we see that our sisters and brothers have fallen into tragedy, yes, we should move to do what we can to help them. And we should do it quickly. But friends, no amount of giving can soothe the heart ache of tragedy. Give and give as you might, you nor I can absolve heart ache. That my friends is a God job.

I don't know why some people endure more pain than others and I don't know why it takes longer for some to heal from pain than others. What I do know is that there is purpose in pain. Sometimes, it is deep pain that pushes us to a level of determination to break from bondage and launch ourselves into a life of freedom. Sometimes, it is deep pain that causes us to have the type of compassion that relates to a sinner's wounds and allows them to see the hope of their promise in the healing of another's wounds. Sometimes, it is pain that crushes us so immensely that the oil of the Lord flows from our lives into another's. And yes, as much as it may hurt and as much as it may even bruise, sometimes pain works in us a good that God can use.

So when viewing another's pain, what if we asked ourselves a question? Are we cutting off the potential for someone's purpose to bloom by trying to rescue them from their pain? And if our answer is yes, then isn't it more loving to walk beside this person while they endure their pain than to recuse them from their pain and cut off their purpose?

Ouch! I know. If you are one of the few people who have learned how to do this with balance, consider yourself wise. It is not easy. And it can oftentimes feel cruel. Well at least it feels that way for me.

When someone I love is in pain, I want them to not be in pain. I want to do anything and everything I can to make their pain stop. And I want them to do anything and everything they can to stop feeling the pain that they feel. It is oh, so hard.

So, where do we find the balance? This may be an easier question to answer. I usually ask myself two questions to help me determine if it is appropriate to enter someone's suffering with a rescue in mind.

Question One – Is this a need I **CAN** meet?

This is a simple question. Do I have what this person needs? If they are in a financial bind, do I have extra resources to give that would help them get to a better place? If they need a friend with a listening ear, am I able to spare an hour or two during the week just to listen to them? If they need a job or a place to stay, am I able to provide employment or shelter?

This may be a sacrifice, but the question is not asking if it will hurt when I do it. Instead, it is asking if I am able to do it. If I cannot answer yes to this question, then their need is either a need that God wants someone else to meet or a need God wants to meet Himself.

Question two – Is this a need I **SHOULD** meet?

This is where things get a little stickier and require thought, prayer, and the leading of the Holy Spirit. But here's one definite I can give myself right from the start. If this is not a need I CAN meet, then this is also not a need that I SHOULD meet. God does not require us to do anything He has not given us resources for. When he required that the widow feed the prophet, she may have given her last, but she had her last to give. (See 1 Kings 17:8-24) But, if my answer to question one is "yes," this is where I really need to use wisdom and the Holy Spirit as a guide.

Sometimes, our hearts are bigger than our resources and we give our all to others leaving ourselves and our family at a deficit. Take some time to pray and really hear God's voice. I do believe that the Holy Spirit sometimes prompts us to give to others out of sacrifice, but when He does, we have the faith and security in knowing that what God has asked us to give by the leading of the Holy Spirit, God will replace by making sure we have what we need.

If we are giving out of our own guilt or our own need to feel needed, we can't depend on that same promise. So, think carefully, pray earnestly, and decide wisely.

Another thing to consider is the reason the need exists. While I am not a big fan of judging someone else's lifestyle, I do think that it is important to hold others accountable for the consequences of their decisions. So, I ask myself a few sub-questions before determining if I should meet the need of another person.

1. Is this a need created by an addiction or pattern of wrong behavior?
2. Is this a need created by a person's deliberate rebellion or negligence?

If the answer to either of these two questions is yes, then I ask myself one last question. Does God desire for me to be an agent of grace and use my resources to help this person? If the answer is no, then I now know that this is not a need I should meet.

But…if the answer is yes, I am led by the Holy Spirit as to how to meet the need and how long I should meet the need. I am God's servant, but I am not God!

And guess what friend, no one else is! No one can be God, but God! But how good it is to know that He is God! And God will never, ever fail us. Even when our pain does happen to be our fault. God's heart for us is so big that He loves us past our mistakes, past our rebellion, and past our pain. Despite what many of us have grown up in church learning, He is a good God! He loves us. He wants to restore us and He wants to bless us!

We should be very glad that the people we look to fail us. Many times it is only when people fail us that we actually turn to the God who NEVER will! And in Him we find limitless love, healing, restoration, safety, security, and provision. He is unfailing!!!

A prayer for you today:

God, the friend reading this really needs Your provision in their life today. I do not know their need, but you do. Father, will you please speak to the heart of my friend today and let them know that YOU are everything that they need! Restore their confidence in your inability to fail at being God and prove yourself to them wherever their life needs Your touch. In your wonderful son Jesus' Name, Amen.

CHAPTER 10

ALL IN HIS HANDS

After dropping my daughter off to school in the morning, it is usually my custom to turn on an inspirational podcast or Christian radio show to help me jumpstart my day with the right focus. So, one morning, I did just that. And I was blown away when the guest that day made a confession that I too held. Her mother had just passed away before the Christmas holiday and she was on the show to talk about grief. The show host asked her where she had the most difficulty being herself. "Church." She abruptly responded. "Church."

I found it interesting. Much like myself, she hadn't just lived her life in church, but she lived her life with Jesus. She loved God. She loved church. She loved people. But she was hurting. And boy do I understand.

Grief takes time. And we don't just grieve when someone dies. We grieve when some**thing** dies. A dream. A business. A marriage. A career. These are all things that can die, and we need to grieve them in order to heal from them.

Our sweet Christian sisters and brothers mean well, but if they have never had a hole in their soul so deep that it cuts through the very core of who they are, they may not understand that you are doing all you can just to hold on to Jesus. They may not understand that you barely made it to church and just need to be able to be your whole self in the presence of Jesus. They may not understand, but God does.

Living through some very dark seasons of life, I have learned something about people. Not just Christian people, but people in general. If they haven't lived in those seasons of deep rooted pain, sadness and sorrow make them uncomfortable. They mean well. But it is easier for them to encourage you to smile than to embrace you or sit with you in your pain. And here's yet another secret. Sitting with you in your pain is harder for people who really love and care for you. Because people who care for you want to see you happy.

I understand that forced happiness is the last thing you need in this moment and I totally empathize with your need to be embraced in your pain. But, there are many people that will never be able to feel the depth of what you feel. They won't understand your pain, but they will feel the helplessness that comes from not being able to change it. So, they say "Smile. The joy of the Lord is your strength."

I have been on the receiving end of such advice just like you and I have wanted so desperately to scream at the person on the other end with berating questions like "Honey, do you know how much I have tried to smile? Do you know how many praise and worship songs I have listened to trying to get my joy back? Do you know how many sacrifices of praise I have brought to the altar? Do you know how many conversations with God I have had asking Him to take my heavy burden and give me a garment of praise?" Don't get me started because I may never stop. I'm sure you can see that I fully understand where you are!

Here's the truth I am living in this season. God gives us joy, peace, love, and all of those wonderful things, but He also gives us long suffering. He gives us temperance. Why? Because He knows there will be times in life where we will need to endure suffering and pain.

The Bible tells us that there is a season for pain and suffering in Ecclesiastes 3. There are many people who know that scripture and recite it often, but they usually use it to tell us that it is time to "get up and be happy." Listen closely to what I am about to say. Do not miss your time of joy stuck in mourning. But when life has ushered you into a season of mourning, do not allow someone else's uncomfortableness to cause you guilt when you are unable to rejoice.

There is a time for everything,
and a season for every activity under the heavens:

a time to be born and a time to die,
a time to plant and a time to uproot,
a time to kill and a time to heal,
a time to tear down and a time to build,
a time to weep and a time to laugh,
a time to mourn and a time to dance

(Ecclesiastes 3: 1-4)

Joy is a beautiful thing. But many times, we fail to see that pain sometimes is just as beautiful. It connects us to God as our comforter. Wounds connect us to God as our mender. Ailments whether they are in the body or in the mind connect us to God as our healer.

If we rush through our season of pain trying to get to joy, we will miss the beauty of putting our every feeling, every longing, and every need into the hands of a capable God who can handle it all.

The Weight of Life

There is a difference between managing the weight of life and carrying the weight of life. Carrying the weight of life slows me down and renders me unable to function. Managing the weight of life teaches me that thriving in the midst of a heavy situation is about carrying only what is assigned to me and dropping the rest at the feet of Jesus. It is about becoming comfortable with the uncomfortable and learning that it is okay to wait on Jesus. I follow peace and am lead by the Holy Spirit. When uncertainty creeps into my heart, I cling closer to the One I know to be secure and I seek Him with my whole heart. He doesn't just have my answer; He is my answer.

I remember a particularly difficult emotional moment in my life where I was desperately seeking joy and happiness. I began rummaging through scriptures believing that if I just got a hold to a few good scriptures about joy, I could begin to declare them over my life and change my mood.

I prayed and asked God to grant me joy and then began to recite those scriptures and declare those things over my life. Even after all of that, I could not shake the sadness that I was feeling. I started to feel like such a horrible Christian and began to ask myself why so many people I know can recite these scriptures and change their moods. It didn't quite work that way for them either, but there goes that broken perspective again.

It was my brokenness, not my elation that gave way to an answer. In my frustration that then led to tears, I began to feel God's comfort and hear his gentle reassuring voice say to me that just as He is my joy, He is also my comforter.

He doesn't want me to dismiss my pain without acknowledging it. Quite the contrary. He wants me to acknowledge my pain and give it to Him. So cry those tears, sweet sister! Wallow in that floor. Do whatever it is you need to do to release those emotions to God. And then let Him replace them with what He's got for you.

God would not have given us so many references in His Word about exchanging what is ours for what is His if He never expected us to have emotions, burdens, and even habits and behaviors that were contrary to His best for us. The key is to make the exchange!

Don't deny your pain, but don't sit in it either. Feel it, release it, and exchange it. Did you just breathe that healing sigh of relief like I did? I sure hope so. Let's do it again, but let's make it personal.

Whatever your emotion or pain is, feel it, release it, and exchange it. Today, my pain is from the uncertain future of my family unit as it exists today. I feel that uncertainty tugging at my heart and I am choosing to release that uncertainty to God. In exchange for my uncertainty, I receive the surety of knowing that God's plans for my future are good. I don't know my future, but He knows. And because He knows, I can rest in the surety of His goodness and His plan.

What did you release into His hands? What did you receive? You may need to release it over and over again until it becomes a settled thing in your spirit. That's okay. Just keep feeling, keep releasing, and keep exchanging!

Your Future

If you are reading this book, chances are that you are a little dreary and uncertain about your future. Let's be real. The title of this book is *Grace in a Shattered Place*. So, it's clear that if you are reading, something in your life is shattered. There are some people who can go along with the free fall of life and totally enjoy it, but if you are like me and like to see where you are going, being in the dark is completely discomforting.

I am not one of those people who had an age, date, and goal

timeline, but I am certainly one of those people who planned her life out in seasons. Yep. I had one of those girly life timelines that sounded something like this. I'm going to graduate school, then go to college and become a doctor. I'm going to get married, have three kids, and then travel the world. My family is going to all love Jesus. We are all going to be dedicated volunteers in our church, have lots of money, and live happily ever after. That's how everyone's life story ends, right?

Okay, grant it. My timeline was very superficial. Give me a break here, would you? I was in high school. By my mid-20's, I created a timeline with a more realistic point of view. Even still, if you were to ask me how far away my life deviated from even this realistic set of goals, you would be amazed! Some things are yet to be seen. But I am not a doctor. I do not have three kids. I have not traveled the world and I have not done a bunch of other things on that list either!

Some deviations are not all bad. I'm not the best at math, so being a doctor of medicine probably wasn't a great career pick. Philosophy maybe. But medicine?? Let's just say that if you were sick and desperately needed a doctor, you would thank God that I wasn't the one he sent! And that's okay. As we grow in Christ, we learn to let go of what He hasn't given us and embrace the things that He has.

My point in all of this is that my life has taken so many turns and twist that my self-created timeline might as well be shredded and thrown in a trash compactor! What's more is that nowhere on my timeline was the season of "sit in the dark and wait." Want to guess what this season of life has me doing? Yep! I am currently sitting in the dark waiting! I guess you could say I'm being led by a flashlight. So while it may not be completely dark, it's still not looking very bright!

I'm sure that season wasn't on your timeline either. But, the lesson to learn in it all is that our future must be in the hands of God. I am totally not saying that we have absolutely no control over what happens with our lives. God certainly isn't going to drop your dream job in your lap and say, "Here! I know you've been dreaming of this ever since you were a child, so I thought I'd just make it happen for you." You can go ahead and wake up from that dream because that's not going to happen either! Blessing without preparation is a disaster waiting to happen!

Here's some reassurance. In those seasons where you are doing all you can and nothing seems to be turning out the way you planned, you can rest knowing that your times and your future are in the hands of God. This frees us from anxiety or what I like to call absent living.

Absent living is the process of being so focused on what you fear will or will not happen in the future that you fail to be present in the moment. Thereby, you completely miss the life you are living in the now. My personal prayer has been that God would wake me up from absent living and cause me to be present in my present. And yes, the wording in that last sentence was intentional!

Want to know what it's going to take for me? The same thing it's going to take for you. You and I both must choose to embrace the now in the midst of an uncertain future. Yes, I know. We feel like we need to know if we will ever get married, ever have children, ever finish school, ever land the career of our dreams, ever travel around the world, ever reconcile that marriage, that friendship, or that family relationship. Otherwise, we will never be able to have peace. Or, will we?

God's answers for us are opposite our own. In Matthew 6:34, He tells us to take no thought about tomorrow, but our minds tend to think way into the next year. In 1 Peter 5:7, He tells us to cast all of our anxieties upon Him, but we tend to roll our anxieties over and over again in our heads until we can find our own solution. It kind of makes me wonder how opposite our lives would be if we actually took the time to apply God's instructions rather than our own default thinking.

What if we actually took the plunge and threw all of our wishes and worries to the side and sought His kingdom first? What if we actually dared to believe that He would keep His Word and add to our lives all of the other things that we've been seeking? Be careful here. That scripture clearly and probably purposely did not say that he would add all the things we dreamed. It said, all **these** things will be added. "These things" are the things that enable us to live a life full of love, joy, and peace – all of the things that are most important in life. Rest assured, it may not be all the things you hoped for, but when you are walking with God, there are bound to be a few surprises along the way that will blow your wish list to shreds!

Your Heart

If you have stuck with me this long, you are well on your way to your place of surrender where your life is truly all in God's hands. Before we close this chapter, there is just one more thing we should talk about. Our hearts.

It amazes me how so many people give their hearts away to people, passions, and things that will never fill them the way God can. We are always searching for something to fill that big empty space in our hearts when the only thing that will satisfy us completely is God's presence.

When I talk about God's presence, I am not referring to the presence that you may feel in church on Sunday morning. I absolutely live for those experiences in corporate worship where the atmosphere is so fully charged with the anointing that His presence almost feels tangible. We need those moments. But that's not what I mean here.

I'm not even referencing a quiet moment between just you and God. You know, one of those moments where you may be sitting in your car pouring your heart out with tears running down your face. Those moments are priceless. But that's still not what I mean here.

I really do mean that choosing to allow God to sit in the empty places of our hearts and fill them with everything that He is, in the place of everything that we have not and everything that we are not, is the only thing that can satisfy that void. It is truly allowing God into the empty places and saying "God, expand and enlarge in my heart until there is only you. Fill every hole and every crevice with your love, your peace, your joy, your laughter, your plan, and your purpose."

When God abides in your heart, He really fills it!! There will be no more feeling empty because you will be filled with so much of His plan and purpose that you will run over!

I know it doesn't feel like it now, but that friends, is where grace comes in. Grace in the moment of despair. Grace in the moment of emptiness. Grace in the moment of pain. Grace in the moment of a desperate ache. Grace in your shattered place.

I promised I wouldn't fill this book with cheesy cliché's. So here is the real truth. Sometimes there is no pretty sentence that will coat your aching heart. God has to do that. Sometimes there is no person that will fill that empty space. God has to be that.

The grace in our shattered places is revealed when we run to Him, embrace Him, and allow our barren places to be filled by Him. Grace mends our shattered places when we fix our eyes on Him and choose to say, God I am lonely, but You are enough. God I am hurting, but You are enough. God I am angry, but You are enough. God I am numb, but You are enough. Your grace is enough. Your plan is enough. Who You are is enough. God I don't know what my tomorrow holds, but I am going to get up, think up, and look up because You are enough.

You and I will find comfort for the deep ache in our souls when we park our hearts in the fullness of His grace. His grace is enough to mend our shattered hearts. It's enough to take the pieces of our shattered lives and breathe into them new hope, new joy, and a new song for our tomorrow.

May His grace resurrect every shattered dream in your life and cause you to live again.

KEEPING IT PRACTICAL

Writing to your heart and soul directly from mine has been one of the most rewarding, yet challenging things that I have ever done. It's easy to write about grace when its beauty is visibly present in the form of victory. But when its beauty is hidden in the dark places of life, it's a much more complex task.

It is my heart's prayer that my truth and transparency became a flashlight shining into your dark cave and provided the encouragement you needed to look up and see the light again. Before I write my last word and punctuate my last sentence, I wanted to share some of the practical things I have personally put to practice in my life as I keep my eyes focused on Jesus and daily make the shift toward His grace.

Accountability

What we least want when we are going through a difficult time is for someone to tell us to get up, get dressed, and get to living. But most times, that is exactly what we need. We need someone who will sit with us in our dark places, but more than that, we need someone who will tell us when we've been there too long!

Seriously. The best thing that God could've ever given me in this season is the two friends who would periodically call me and ask, "So, what are you doing today?" Initially, I thought they were asking because they had made plans and wanted me to come join them.

Sometimes, that actually was the case, but more often than not, they really meant, "So, what are YOU doing today?" That was their way of saying, "Look. You are going to have to get up and shake this off of you. You are going to have to get back to life no matter how difficult and no matter how hard.

In the beginning, they were willing to make suggestions and even come along with me. But as time moved on, they stopped being so gentle. A picture posted on one of my social media pages came from one of those not so gentle times. It's a picture of my sweet baby girl sitting on a pumpkin in the middle of a pumpkin patch. The story behind the picture came from an assignment one of my friends gave me. "I don't care what you do today," she said. "But you have to get up! Get out and do something with that baby girl and I want to see a picture!" She was serious and so I obliged!

While it's laughable now, I have to confess something to you about how I felt then. I thought my friends were really being hard on me. After all, my life had just taken a huge hit. I really felt like they should've let me stay home and lay across my bed in the dark. But if they had not pushed me, I might still be sitting at the bottom of that pit.

Church activities, workout sessions, and music lessons are some of the other ways that I have continued to make myself accountable. These are things that I enjoy, but they are also added commitments that require me to be in a certain place at a certain time doing a certain thing. Service to others and self-improvement is a wonderful way to keep my focus in perspective.

Media Filtering

This was a hard one for me. I don't watch much television, but the shows that I do watch, I really love to watch! Having to cut out those scandalous and sometimes steamy drama television shows that I specifically blocked time out of my schedule on a certain day of the week to watch was so very hard.

Even harder than that was hearing my friends have a conversation about those same shows the day after they aired. I know I don't have to even explain. We've all been there. And don't let there have been a dramatic plot twist that we happen to miss! It's almost like we've missed out on a part of the world and our minds are eager to find out what exactly happened to stir up such conversation.

So, you can see. I'm definitely not saying that this was the easiest thing to do, but it was necessary. At least in the very beginning. I was serious about getting up from the dark place that I was in, so I wasn't going to bank my healing on how stable my wavering emotions would be one episode to the next while I watched other peoples' fantasy careers, homes, and relationships all flash before my eyes. Nope! I wasn't willing to risk it. So I walked away. For a season.

As my healing progresses, I am beginning to add some of those things back in my life, but I have a strong gage on how much is too much. If something I watch or listen to starts to affect me emotionally, I identify the source and back away from it until I am able to handle it.

Limit Social Media

Yes, I know that social media is a form of a media and could've been added into that last section, but since it is so prevalent in our present culture, I felt that I needed to isolate it and address it by itself.

Here's the truth. I love social media! It connects me to distant family, old classmates, friends, and people in my church and community. Not to mention, there are tons of recipes, do it yourself ideas, business tools, promotional avenues, and virtual support groups. Social media has so many positive uses. But, there are some negative things to be aware of, too.

One glaring negative is that social media promotes superficial comparison in a way that's never been possible before. Yes, people compared themselves before social media platforms ever existed. And yes, they still compare themselves outside of social media. All of this is true.

Now however, there is an added in your face shiny and glittery perfection on social media pages that makes someone else's life look so much better than ours. And the opposite is true as well. Let's not be unwise here. There is always someone who has it a little worse than we do. And to them, the shiny and glittery perfection of our social media pages is that filtered perfection they long for.

When our perspective is balanced, we can engage in social media in a way that allows us to keep in contact with extended family members and friends, celebrate the accomplishments of others, and even provide words of encouragement and support to someone going through a difficult time.

However, when I was thrown off kilter by yet another life torpedo, I noticed that my perspective about the things that I saw on social media was not balanced at all. I looked at the shiny images of made up people with smiles and started to wonder what was wrong with me that I couldn't have the happy life that they seemed to have.

All the while, I was oblivious to the fact that I too, put up nice, shiny pictures of myself on social media. I don't want the pictures of myself that I put on social media to show me with my hair uncombed, wearing torn pajamas, and looking like I haven't showered in two weeks. For Pete's sake, my mama and daddy raised me better than that! So, I choose pictures that show me at my best. The person looking at that picture can't tell if I was crying just before I snapped that selfie any more than they can tell if a family was arguing in a car moments before their photographer snapped that perfect family photo.

I'm not saying that everyone forces themselves to smile in their pictures. I'm also not saying that no one is ever genuinely happy. What I am saying however, is that what social media gives us is a single snap shot. One single snap shot of one single moment.

A string of single life snapshots or a string of single moments in a person's day is never enough for us to know the totality of someone else's life.

I try my best to be honest about both my highs and lows on social media. But even in my honesty, there is some truth that I hold back because social media isn't an intimate setting between my family and closest friends. It is a snap shot profile available on the internet for all to see. What you see online cannot be used as a measuring stick to evaluate the happiness in that other person's life. Similarly, it cannot be used as a measuring stick to evaluate the happiness or lack of happiness in your own life. Truth has to do that. God's truth.

When I found myself caught up in the comparison trap of social media, I had to set some parameters in place to keep the highlight reel from consuming my thoughts. For a short period of time, I backed away completely in order to realign my perspective. Then, I set a few strict guidelines to govern how I interacted on social media. I will share them with you now.

Rule #1

I will not allow social media to be the first thing I see in the morning or the last thing I see at night.

Okay, truth told, this should have been my rule all along. But it's so easy to fall into the trap of rolling over and checking my phone before getting out of bed in the morning or mindlessly scrolling through my timeline before bed at night. I had to make a commitment to myself that I would begin my day and end my day focusing on God's truths.

Rule # 2

I will only log into social media on one device

This was my way of keeping social media in its place. I would not allow myself to toggle from phone to tablet or computer to phone checking social media. This is how I disciplined myself to govern my use of social media and not allow social media to govern me.

Rule #3

If at any time, I find myself comparing someone's highlight to my reality, I will log off of social media immediately

No explanation needed.

Rule #4

I will stop the use of social media by 10:30pm every night.

Honest moment. I don't always follow these rules exactly as they are written now. I have adjusted them as I have become more balanced in my perspective, but for the most part, these are the rules I adhere to. Feel free to steal them and alter them for yourself as you see fit.

Before we move on, may I say one last thing about social media? It is not a substitute for real connection. Yes, we get to see a glimpse into the lives of people we are distant from, but we can't hear the sound of their voices. And we don't get to feel the joy and warmth of their presence through our computers and mobile devices. Only true sound, presence, and touch can do that. Let's not allow social media to become a replacement for real connection. Let's visit and call more often than we message and post.

Worship

I was having a conversation with my Pastor's wife who happens to be one of the sweetest and most giving women you will ever meet. She also happens to be the worship Pastor at our church. Anyway, during our conversation, I shared with her some of the things that I had been praying for. "Prayer is good." She said. "But prayer is a lot of us talking to God and thinking about what to say and ask for next. Worship allows us to hear and receive from God." She has never been more right.

Worship has unequivocally been the most powerful tool that has helped me in this season. I think it is important for me to share that even though I love to worship and love to sing songs of worship, I found it hard to enter into a place of worship during this season. It was not easy to push past what I was feeling to see Jesus. For a while, it seemed that the darkness around me literally blocked my view of His glory.

I had to make a conscious effort to worship God even while I was hurting. I know that's something you have heard before. Probably spoken from a pulpit. So, I'm going to walk you through the practicality of what my choice looked like in a few stages.

Stage 1:
Honest communication with God that sounds like this -

God, I don't feel like worshipping today, but I know that You are the only way out of my situation. So I am going to make the choice to worship anyway. Lord, I love you. I magnify you. I lift You. You are worthy.

I don't really feel connected to the words I am saying at this stage, but I am deciding to speak the truth of who God is until my heart catches up to what my mouth is declaring.

Stage 2:

I still don't feel like worshipping, but I take ten minutes out of my day to play my worship music and focus on God. Something in the music breaks through the hardness of my heart and I began to sing and lift my hands

Stage 3:

Honest Communication that sounds like this:

God, I thank you that there was a breaking in my spirit as I committed to getting in your presence. Today, I worship you because here is where I find my life and my peace.

This time, my heart is aligned with the words coming out of my mouth. I can see God's greatness and I begin to worship freely.

I'm not really sure whether or not this took three days or thirty. I'm not even sure this happened in three stages. I just wanted to show that although I didn't feel God's presence in the beginning, the more I spoke of His presence and sat in His presence, the more His presence cut through the hard places of my heart. The more I worshipped, the more I saw things differently.

Prayer is important, but if I only pray and neglect worship, my focus is only on the things that I would like for God to do that He hasn't yet done. When I worship, my focus is on that fact that God is so much bigger than those needs and desires.

In fact, there is so much wrapped up in Him and being in His presence that those things don't even matter. Yes, I want that financial breakthrough. I want that relationship to be restored. I want that sickness to be healed. I want that job promotion. I want my child to be delivered. But my fulfillment is not in the answered prayer. My fulfillment is in the God of the answer.

Focus on the End Result

It was so easy to say that I was a vessel for Christ and that my life was not about my own personal gain until the storms of life came. Then, I forgot all about being a surrendered vessel for Christ. I forgot all about living for His glory. Life became about my comfort, my pleasure, and my plan. But God did not create me so that He could fulfill my needs and follow my plans. He created me so that I could meet His needs by giving Him worship and fulfill His plan.

When I keep this in mind and purposely hit my knees in a surrendered posture, I tell God that I only want Him to be glorified. Seeking to glorify Him does two things. It frees me from the pressure of trying to figure out how things will turn out, and it allows me to rest knowing that the outcome will only be good.

Good doesn't mean just as I want it. Good means just as He wants it. Good means that things will turn out so right that they will bring Him glory.

The middle may be dark, but if I lose in the end, God is not glorified. That's not His way. That's not His plan.

God wants to do something so great in us and for us that it will cause us and the others around us to turn and give Him glory. He wants others to see His greatness. His power. His might. He wants the glory.

Knowing that God wants to get glory out of my life frees me from worrying about being left for dead in the darkness of this pit because I know that His glory shines when He lifts me and as He lifts me.

So, last word. Last sentence. Last prayer. God, be glorified!

PRAYERS AND REFLECTIONS

When Life Is Unfair

God, I know life is not fair, but you are the healer of broken hearts. You will not let everything that I put into this area of my life be a waste. The seeds that I have sown, you will allow me to reap. Please help me to hold on through this unfair season in my life. Please hear my heart in this very difficult place. I know that you love me and I know that you are carrying me. Please allow this pain to transform me into something great and something beautiful for Your Kingdom. Amen.

When You Need to Strengthen Your Faith

God, help me to exercise and walk in the faith and trust that I have in You even when my world is falling apart. I know that you love me and You will never forsake or abandon me. Help me to hold on to this truth when I am believing for what seems impossible. I fully trust You. Amen.

When You Are Praying for Restoration

God, I believe that it is Your will for (name what you are believing God to restore) to be restored in my life. I am bringing it to the foot of the cross knowing that you are able and have all Power in your hands.

You are a restorer. You can take broken pieces and replace them with something new. Even though I am hurting, I know that You can do far more than I can ever imagine. I receive the restoration of (insert your need) In Jesus Name. Amen.

When You Need to Rest in God

Lord, quiet my thoughts with Your pure, true, steadfast, and unchanging Word. Help me to find my joy and complete peace in You. Help me to let go of what I am holding on to, so that You can have it. Help me to worship You wholly, withholding nothing. Help me to truly give those things that are God things over to You. My career. My dreams. My marriage. My finances. My parenting. My friendships. Help me to leave those at the foot of the cross. Help me to trust and rely on Your guidance. Help me to hear your voice clearer and louder than any outside voice. If You speak it, I will do it. Help me to walk in the peace and confidence of Your word. I give every fear over to You. You are a good God. You would not cause me harm. If something is broken in my life, You have a resolution. Even in moments when I am hurting and unsure, help me to worship You. Let my worship be pure. Help me to worship You as the answer and not just for the answer. In the midst of chaos and confusion, help me to keep my eyes on you. Be my stability. Help me rest in You. You created me to be yours first. Your praise. Your worship. You said that you would grant me the desires of my heart. You are working for me. Your angels are warring on my behalf. Thank you for the victory!! I praise you for You are too wise to ever make a mistake. You hear every prayer and You answer!! Amen.

When You Are Struggling
with Disappointment

Lord, please empty me of me. Dig deep inside of me to those feelings of resentment, disappointment, hurt, anger, and pain and replace them with feelings of forgiveness, feelings of grace, and feelings of love. I don't understand this part of my life, but you do. You have not forgotten me. You see just where I am. You see my heart to please you. Help me to hold on to these truths when I am feeling the bitterness of my position in life. Heal me from thoughts and feelings of rejection and deliver me from the trap of comparison. Help me to find my security in Your Word. You are faithful to Your Word. You will heal my heart. I will breathe easy and free when I live in Your presence. You are not finished healing me. You will not leave me broken, bitter, and dejected. God, I trust You to be my healer. Make me something beautiful. Let every broken piece fit together into the masterpiece you have created. The Glory is Yours. Always and Forever. Amen.

When You Need to Forgive
Those That Didn't Help

God, only You are holy and all knowing. Only you can fully discern the heart and issues of a man. Only You have the ability to hear all request at one time and not be overwhelmed, not miss a thing, not overlook an issue, and not see a heart. So first, I ask your forgiveness for putting that burden and responsibility on others. You are the only God. Others may have the heart to help, but they are human just like I am. They are flawed just like I am. They have issues just like I have issues. They have limitations just like I have limitations. God, I release other people from the burden I have placed on them. They are your vessels, but they are not You. I have missed the needs of others before. I have misjudged hearts. I have ignored a cry for help. Lord, help me to view people in a balanced way. Help me to realize that even when the hearts of others are genuine, they are flesh and can never do what You can. Help me to run to You first for my needs. Lord, please take the seat that I have given others in my life away and build your throne. Father, forgive me for holding anger and resentment toward others and help me to forgive myself for my unbalanced reliance on them. They are not God. You are! Thank You for perfecting and restoring my life. In Jesus' Name, Amen!

ACKNOWLEDGEMENT

To my husband and best friend, Mario, I can't say thank you enough for trusting me to share small parts of our mud with others, even while we are still in our middle. Thank you for your love, encouragement, and consistent support. To my girls, Nyla and Aleah, one cheering from heaven and the other cheering from the room across the hall, you both make my heart beam with joy! To my parents, family, friends, and church family, thank you so much for your continuous love and support! I love you all!

Printed in the United States
By Bookmasters